THE INCREDIBLE T-6 PILOT MAKER

Walt Ohlrich and Jeff Ethell

Specialty Press

First published in the U.S. 1983 by
Specialty Press Publishers and Wholesalers, Inc.
Box 426
Osceola, WI 54020

ISBN 0-933424-34-5

Printed in the U.S.A.
10 9 8 7 6 5 4 3 2 1

First U.K. Edition published 1983 by
Midland Counties Publications (aerophile) Limited
24 The Hollow, Earl Shilton, Leicester, LE9 7NA U.K.

ISBN 0-904597-46-6 in the U.K.

The Flying Instructor's Prayer

My student is a headache that I do not want.
He maketh me to lie down at night very weary.
He leadeth me beside high tension wires.
Yea, though he knoweth better, my hair turneth gray.
And though I fly on the clearest days,
I fear much evil, for he is with me. Amen.

Courtesy of Arthur O. Houston
USAAF P-47 Thunderbolt pilot

Table of Contents

ACKNOWLEDGEMENTS 5

PREFACE 6

FORWORD 6

CHAPTER ONE North American Earns Its Spurs 8

CHAPTER TWO Naval Aviators and J-Birds 19

CHAPTER THREE Hot Rock Pilots and Terrible Texans . 68

CHAPTER FOUR Flight Lieutenants and Harvards 115

CHAPTER FIVE THE TEXAS FLIES ON 137

VERSION TABLE 142

GLOSSARY 143

BIBLIOGRAPHY 144

Acknowledgements

Though the authors get the credit, no book of this nature is possible without the generous help of fellow historians and former participants. All of you who pitched in made the long hidden story of the Texan come alive, a story that had been waiting to be told.

Each official agency was eager to open their files: Office of Naval Aviation History, Magazines & Books Division of the USAF Office of Public Affairs, USAF 1361st Photo Squadron, Defense Audio Visual Agency, Office of Air Force History, Albert F. Simpson Historical Research Center.

Our fellow historians were continually opening their files without hesitation: American Aviation Historical Society Negative Lending Library, Dusty Carter, Pete Bowers, Harry Gann, Hal Andrews, Bill Larkins, Dr. William Armstrong, Bob Blakie, Santiago Flores Ruiz, Bernie Karsh, Jerry Walbrun, Fred G. Krapf III, Wilton, H. Clary, Sol Cohen, Norm Avery, Norm Taylor, Norm Malayney, John Underwood, Roger Besecker, Dave Menard, Clarence Simonsen, W. Eckersley, Ken Sumney, Dewitt Brewer, Jim Sullivan, Phil Edwards at the National Air & Space Museum, Fred Johnsen, Dana Bell, Dick Phillips, Gene Chase—EAA & Warbirds of America.

And, of course, without those of you who took part in the aircraft's history first hand, the book would have been woefully incomplete, for after all, it is your story: A. J. Bibee, Maj, USMC (Ret); Charles J. "Obie" O'Brien, Cdr, USN (Ret); Chet Bartusiak, Capt, USNR (Ret); Len Cobb; John P. Vivian; Robert G. Schipf, Lt., USNR (Ret); Jack V. Hoey, Cdr. USNR (Ret); Mark O. Shriver, Capt, USNR (Ret); Pete Vandersluis; Tom Woolcock, Capt, USN (Ret); Marvin M. Quaid, Cdr, USN (Ret); Tom Schaaf, Cdr, USN (Ret); H. W. "Hec" Davis, Capt, USN (Ret); W. F. Short, LCdr, USN (Ret); William E. Scarborough, Capt, USN (Ret); Robert E. Dixon, RAdm, USN (Ret); S. M. Shelton, Cdr, USN (Ret); James A. Mulligan, Capt, USN (Ret); Don Wernimont, Cdr, USN (Ret); Paul A. Ludwig, Cdr, USN (Ret); Al K. McDonald, Col, USAF (Ret); Ken Hamilton; Jeff Brown; Charlie Hubbs; Geoff Hirons, Flt Lt, RAF (Ret); R. W. Swift, F/O, RCAF (Ret); Gerold Bickley, Col, USAF (Ret); John Peters; William Mann, CWO-3, USAF (Ret); Eugene Gauch, BGen, USAF (Ret); Frank Barry; Richard Woodhull, Jr., Col, USAF; Dick Mottern; C. L. Weidinger, Col, USAF; Vernon "Bud" Hesterman; Harold Scott; Thomas Dorsey, Maj, USAF (Ret); A. L. Young, Col, USAF (Ret); Jack Gale; J. T. Pace; John B. McMaster; Walt Allen; Chester Marshall; Carroll R. Anderson; William Koerschner, Jr., Col, USAF (Ret); E. R. Beard; Dave Leonard; Bernard Marsh; Kermit Mathison; Sidney Smith; Lawrence Goldwasser; Robert Moore; Arthur O. Houston; Schlomo Nir, Lt Col, Israel Air Force; Francis "Curley" Satterlee; Robert Anderson; David L. Hudson, Sqdrn Ldr, RAAF (Ret); Jack Ilfrey; J. F. Carter; William J. Reedy; Robb Satterfield; Don Contact; Robert Jones, Jr.; Edward Zappen; Richard Suter; R. M. Tvede, Jr., Cdr, USN (Ret); George Collinge; Lloyd Royer; Thomas Kolk; John A. deVries, Col, USAF (Ret); Ed Damico; Chester Marshall; Gary Sparks, Maj, USAF (Ret); T. O. Thompson; John Most; Andy Henry, Lt Col, USAF (Ret).

Without question the book could never have been completed without the generous support and direct help of our wives, Jeanne G. Ohlrich and Bettie T. Ethell—for both of you to put up with us only deepens our love for you.

And to all of our fellow Texan and Harvard pilots, past and present, and in particular to those who fly with us as members of Warbirds of America, may this effort do justice to one fine airplane.

Walt Ohlrich & Jeff Ethell, 1981

Preface

Just a few days after arrival for Advanced at Selma, Alabama, Class 43-I and with only a few hours logged in the AT-6 and with no aerobatic time, an Air Inspector came into our ready room looking for a victim. Student officers were always fair game, and this time I was it. This lieutenant colonel wasn't very big—he must have stood on tip toes to pass the physical—but he made up for lack of size in his attitude; he was all spit and polish, brisk, and down to business. Rumor had it that he was a West Point graduate.

The plane assigned to us unfortunately had a faulty intercom—I could only catch every third or fourth word. Since the Colonel had explained what I was to do while we were still on the ground, the bad communication wasn't evident until we were up in the air. I was to break out of the pattern, climb to 5,000 feet, and start doing slow rolls. I slopped through two or three when he blew his stack in disgust. He tried to explain over the radio, and finally had to resort to hollering. He finally grabbed the controls and put us through an 8-point slow roll. He yelled back, "Now that's the way to fly a plane!" It *was* beautiful.

Since the intercom was so bad, there wasn't any point in staying up, so he shouted for me to take it back home. So, back to the pattern. While I was on final, I thought I sensed his feet on the pedals and his hand on the stick. "Okay, if he wants to land, let him"—and I put my feet on the floor and my hand in my lap. We made the smoothest, sweetest landing I'd ever experienced, and as soon as we touched down, my feet and hands were back on the job. I taxied in, climbed out, and waited for the expected tongue-lashing concerning my so-called aerobatics. He didn't even look at me—but as he walked back to the ready room he was shaking his head. At last he said, "Lieutenant, you can't do acrobatics for sour apples, but you can sure land an airplane!" Well, someone did, and it wasn't me—if it wasn't the Colonel, that AT-6 must have landed itself—they always said a plane flies better hands off!

THAT was flying the AT-6
as Lawrence Goldwasser
remembered it!

Foreword

For such a significant aircraft, North American Aviation's advanced trainer spawned from the NA-16 of 1935 has been forced to bask in the reflected glory of the great combat aircraft of World War II, particularly from its younger brothers, the P-51 Mustang and the B-25 Mitchell. Trainers rarely receive notoriety for the yeoman service they perform in getting pilots ready for the "hot ships" down the road.

The AT-6, as it was known in the U.S. Army Air Force, SNJ to the Navy, Harvard in the Royal Air Force, has become something of an enigma. Throughout its service life it was either loved or intensely disliked since it was a demanding aircraft with the handling characteristics of a fighter.

Looking at the historical record, the AT-6 was one of the more important aircraft to come out of the late 1930s. Few, if any, realized that upon this single type, more than any other, the entire Allied war effort would depend for well trained combat pilots who would subdue well trained, well equipped enemies around the globe. When World War II started, the aircraft was ready for the monumental training tasks required of it/if it had not been safe, reliable, challenging then it would not have been able to perform the mission expected of it when there was simply not enough time to design and develop a new advanced training airplane to teach the masses of Allied pilots needed to fight a war.

The ruggedness and versatility of the Texan, as it later became known, enabled it to become the most widely used training aircraft in history. The airframe was adaptable enough to teach carrier landings, aerial fixed gunnery, glide bombing, flexible hand-held gunnery, aerial photography and instrument flying, not to mention advanced military flying.

For almost two decades it taught American military pilots how to fly and it still serves in the '80s with several air arms. The historical record of what the AT-6 accomplished has been shrouded long enough.

The Flying Instructor's Lament

"What did you do in the war, daddy?
and how did you help to win?"
"Stalls and climbs, Laddy, and
how to get out of a spin.
Woe and Alack, and misery me,
I trundle around in the sky
and instead of machine gunning the enemy
I'm teaching young hopefuls to fly.
Thus is my service rewarded,
My years of experience repaid.
Never a Jap have I followed right down
nor ever gone out on a raid.
They don't ever let us go crazy,
we have to be safe and sedate.
So it's nix on inverted approaches,
they stir up the Major's hate.
And what will the Colonel think?
But we never get sent to pursuit,
we just get a spell in the Link.
So it's a stall and a turn from
morn till night,
and instrument flying till tea.
'Hold 'er off, give her bank,
put your landing gear down.
You're slipping, you're skidding!'
AND THAT'S WHAT I DID IN THE WAR, LADDY."

Chapter One

North American Earns Its Spurs

The founding and management of aviation companies in the 1930s was fraught with continual mergers, sales and changes as visionaries sought to establish their aeronautical dreams on the quicksand of the Depression. In the midst of this milieu, North American Aviation, Inc. (NAA for short) emerged from being a holding company for several different aeronautical firms. It set about constructing its own aircraft when General Motors Corporation ended up with 29 percent of the company in 1933.

North American Aviation gathered its manufacturing section by setting up General Aviation Corp., which became the General Aviation Manufacturing Corporation located in the former Curtiss-Caproni factory at Dundalk, Maryland. In December 1934 the new company, which had yet to design an airplane, came under the presidency of James H. "Dutch" Kindelberger who had been chief engineer for Donald Douglas. With him came John Leland Atwood, another Douglas engineer. These two men would form the heart of NAA through 1962 and it was their expertise that turned the company into a major design and production facility under the name of North American. General Aviation was renamed the Manufacturing Division of NAA, boasting a total of 75 employees.

By the time Kindelberger arrived, the small firm had built several other companies' designs under contract and the prototype of the GA-15 (standing for General Aviation), a military observation aircraft which would later be known as the O-47. Kindelberger and Atwood decided that the company would go after the military market through a specific U.S. Army Air Corps requirement for a basic trainer. It would be upon this aircraft that North American would make a name for itself . . . or continue to struggle.

Kindelberger and Atwood had less than nine weeks to get a prototype to Wright Field, Ohio, for trials in the Basic Trainer Competition. The team stuck with Kindelberger's concept of an airplane that would be easily maintained but a departure from the biplanes of the era. The NA-16 emerged as an all-metal, low wing monoplane with open cockpits in tandem, a fixed landing gear and powered by a 400 hp Wright R-975 radial engine. The only departure from an all-metal configuration was fabric to cover the steel tube fuselage.

On April 1, 1935, famous test pilot Eddie Allen (later killed testing the B-29) took X-2080, the prototype NA-16, into the air over Dundalk for the first time. The same month the NA-16 was flown to Wright where it won the competition, although the AAC requested several modifications, including enclosed cockpits. With an order from the Army for 42 examples of the trainer, under the designation BT-9, NAA faced another major change with a move to California where a factory was being constructed adjacent to Mines Field in Los Angeles. Raymond H. Wright also joined the team as Chief of Stress and Design.

As the factory went up, the production line for the BT-9 was started and NAA test pilot Balfour flew the first example, serial number 36-28, on April 15, 1936, just a year after the prototype had flown. The new aircraft was found to have vicious wing tip stall characteristics, solved to some degree by the addition of slats on the outboard landing edge sections of the wings. The Air Corps wasted little time in ordering 40 more examples as BT-9As (NA-19A) with each carrying a gun camera, one forward and one rear flexible .30 caliber gun. The wing tip stall problem was solved by a two degree washout built into the outer wing panels. The fuselage was lengthened five inches to provide better stability.

One BT-9 was pulled from the assembly line and modified as the NA-22, a primary trainer, but it was later modified back to BT-9 standards. In 1937, 117 BT-9Bs (NA-23) were ordered with minor changes and later in the year 67 BT-9Cs (NA-29) were ordered for the Air Corps Reserve program. One was completed as the BT-9D with redesigned wing panels and tail but the significant change was the first off the line, the Y1BT-10.

Opposite page top to bottom

First of the Many—the NA-16 at Logan Field, Baltimore in 1935 with a civil registration number. The aircraft was painted "Army" blue and yellow in hopes of a military contract and was powered by a Wright R-975. *(Pete Bowers)*

The forerunner of the BT-9 was the NA-18, which was the NA-16 modified to Army specifications with enclosed cockpits, wheel fairings and a Pratt & Whitney engine. *(Pete Bowers)*

The first BT-9 (36-28) off the line and the first North American Aviation aircraft manufactured for the military at Inglewood, California, the company's new factory. *(Cooke via Pete Bowers)*

X-2080

X-2080

An Army Air Corps cadet from Randolph Field, Texas, then called "West Point of the Air," gets his first taste of Basic Training in mid-1940 at the controls of a BT-9. *(A. Dewitt Brewer)*

The U.S. Navy had long realized its need for a monoplane with an enclosed cockpit which could be used for instrument training, instrument flying being a new aspect of flight training with great importance for the future. The BT-9 was of interest to the Bureau of Aeronautics (BuAer) but it never quite came up to Navy standards and the R-975 was not in the Navy's standard engine inventory. BuAer wanted a "Navy engine"—a Pratt & Whitney.

NAA did not want to lose the possibility of extensive Navy sales, particularly since their product was one of the most modern flying. With their own funds they mated a 500 hp P&W R-1340-41 to the first BT-9C airframe and called it the Y1BT-10 as a part of the Army contract. This was the first combination of what would foster over 17,000 examples of the most famous training aircraft ever built, with another 4,500 being built under license in four other countries.

With fiscal year 193738 funds available, the Navy ordered 40 examples of the NJ-1 (NA-28) in late 1936 with 500 hp R-1340-6 Wasp engines and the first airframes came off the Inglewood assembly line in July 1937. The last NJ-1 was tested with a Ranger 550 hp XV-770-4 inline air cooled engine, carrying the NJ-2 designation, but it did not prove practical and the aircraft was remodified to be delivered as an NJ-1.

The Pratt & Whitney/North American combination was obviously agreeing with the services. When the Air Corps ordered the BT-9D with a 450 hp R-985-25 (NA-58), it made one of the largest purchases of training aircraft at the time—251 aircraft would carry the BT-14 designation with new outer wing panels and tail, and a metal covered fuselage. With the R-985-11 engine, 27 were converted to the BT-14A.

The original NA-16 was also modified to carry the P&W R-1340 engine, along with faired landing gear, in which form it was eventually sold to Argentina, but not before beginning a significant part of NAA's business through 1945. Numerous NA charge numbers were assigned to airframes built for overseas export. China, Honduras, Sweden, Australia, Japan, Brazil, France, Britain and other countries bought training and combat versions of the fixed gear, and later retractable gear, NA-16. The RAF turned its examples over to the RCAF as the Yale.

With Dutch Kindelberger selling his products to a pleased Army Air Corps, he and AAC Chief Henry H. "Hap" Arnold formed a working relationship that would carry them through World

War II. The two often bypassed the normal government bog of red tape to get things done and their first try at it was to be very significant indeed, resulting in what was essentially to become the AT-6, SNJ and Harvard series of aircraft.

Ken Hamilton, who began at NAA with some detail drafting on BT-9 components, recalls that "Dutch Kindelberger met with Gen. Hap Arnold and went over a proposal for new trainer aircraft with Hap in a hotel room. Hap listened with interest, and upon conclusion of the presentation, said to Dutch that the airplane looked great,

Virtually a BT-9, but powered by a P&W R-1340-9, the NJ-1 was ordered by the Navy to usher in the monoplane era. This is the first example built, actually patterned on the AAC BT-9C, rolled out on June 20, 1937. *(Norm Avery)*

One of the NJ-1s which came out of the batch of 40 ordered by the USN through the USAAC, the beginning of a long Army/Navy cooperation on North American's trainer series. *(Norm Avery)*

The NA-57 was a French export version of the BT-9B, one of the many overseas export examples of what began with the NA-16. *(Norm Avery)*

The first BC-1 was built for Canada as the NA-26, incorporating all the essential features that would mark the series of trainers from this point on—retractable landing gear, a P&W R-1340 engine and a long greenhouse canopy. *(Dusty Carter/ AAHS)*

The NA-33 was basically the BC-1 set up for production in Australia as the Wirraway. *(Norm Avery)*

that he wanted and needed it in the worst way, but he didn't have any trainer money, every red cent of USAAC money being earmarked for combat aircraft. Without missing a beat, Dutch is said to have responded, 'Hap, you must have misunderstood . . . these aren't trainers, these are Basic *Combat* aircraft (they would have a fixed .30 firing forward, a swivel .30 in the rear)! Hap is said to have responded, 'Why, of course, how dense of me' and the Basic Combat class was born and an order was placed!"

The resultant 1937 Army Circular Proposal 37-220 ordered a competition for a Basic Combat aircraft, a new category that would incorporate armament to approximate front line machines. NAA added retractable landing gear through the talents of Lloyd Royer and designated the prototype as the NA-26. Resulting performance was outstanding and the AAC bought 180 of the aircraft under the designation BC-1 (NA-36). Of this total, 36 were equipped as instrument trainers (BC-1I) and the last three became BC-2s (NA-54).

With license production of the NA-16 already set up in Australia (as the NA-32) the wheels were set up to ship the second example as the NA-33, essentially the BC-1, in September 1937. Commonwealth Aircraft Corporation acquired the right to build both NA-33s and P&W R-1340s under license, with the first plant opening in late 1937. The first Australian-built NA-33 was flown on March 27, 1939, as the Wirraway, an Australian aboriginal word meaning challenger. The fuselage had been strengthened, two forward firing .303s were installed in the upper fuselage and the bomb racks were moved outside the propeller arc to allow the aircraft to dive bomb. A total of 755 were built, with many serving in front line combat during the early portions of the Pacific War. The "Wirra" continued to serve as a trainer until 1959.

On February 11, 1938, Paul Balfour took the first BC-1 into the air, just one day after Louis Wait had flown the first BT-14. In going through the progression of NAA's trainers, it is obvious that many were being developed simultaneously rather than in an orderly fashion one after the other. This often renders the series confusing, with NA numbers and types changing places out of sequence. North American was struggling to get a large slice of the military pie by taking one basic design and exploiting it to the fullest, from trainer, to fighter, to attack bomber. After all, it was upon this single aircraft that Kindelberger would build his reputation, leading to orders for genuine fighter and bomber types.

Beefing up the NA-33, North American immediately pressed forward with the NA-44, "a light Attack Dive-Bomber available for export with unrestricted pursuit plane maneuvers" as the NAA brochure described it after its first flight by Vance Breese in 1938. This time the aircraft was powered by a Wright R-1820-F52 Cyclone of 775 hp and a three bladed propeller, boasting a top speed of 250 mph, loaded for bear. The brochure continued with the following armament description:

> The airplane has provisions for a total of four fixed machine guns, two synchronized with engine and one in each outboard wing. Ammunition boxes have a capacity of 500 rounds for synchronized guns and 275 rounds for wing guns. Also provisions are made for a flexible rear gun installation with a track-type mount. . . .
>
> The gun mounts . . . are designed for installation of: Colt and Browning .30 caliber, .303 caliber, 7 mm, 7.65 mm, 7.9 mm.
>
> The bomb racks, of North American design, are located on the lower surface of each outer wing panel. . . . Bombs may be released selectively from the right or left racks or may be released simultaneously. Bomb carrying capacity: 2-100 pound bombs per rack—4 per ship or 5-24 pound bombs per rack—10 per ship or 3-30 pound bombs per rack—6 per ship.

With the NA-44, North American developed a light attack version of the NA-33 with major improvements, including a Wright R-1820 775 hp engine and an all metal fuselage. Engineering done with this aircraft was passed on to improve the trainer versions of the design. Here the NA-44 is being demonstrated at Floyd Bennett Field, Brooklyn. *(Bachmann via Pete Bowers)*

After demonstrating the NA-44 to several potential customers, Siam ordered 10 as the NA-69 in November 1939, Brazil bought 30 NA-72s and Chile 12 NA-74s in 1940. By July of that year both Brazil and Chile were receiving their aircraft but the Japanese attacked Siam before their aircraft could arrive and the USAAC requisitioned them enroute through the Philippines on board ship. Given the designation A-27, the 10 aircraft were appropriated by Gen Douglas MacArthur's command in the Pacific. The original NA-44 demonstrator ended up in Canada on August 23, 1940, and was not stricken until February 1947.

Pressing on with another export version, North American developed a single seat fighter with a shorter wing and the R-1820-77 of 870 hp, carrying two .30 caliber Colt guns in the cowl and 550 pounds of bombs, with 170 U.S. gallons of fuel. Paul Balfour made the first flight on August 1, 1938. Peru ordered seven NA-50s, which saw some action in 1941 during the war with Ecuador. Six NA-68 versions were ordered by Thailand with modified landing gear, the more angular rather than rounded tail and two 22 mm cannons in fairings under the wings. Completed in November 1940, the NA-60s were absorbed by the U.S. due to Japanese hostile moves toward the Thais and they ended up in Army advanced fighter transition during the war as P-64s.

Impressed with the Yale, the British wanted an advanced trainer similar to the BC-1 and NAA was only too happy to oblige with the Harvard I (NA-49), a BC-1 with British-specified equipment. Ken Hamilton was assigned as lead engineer on the Harvard I and II power plant installations. "On the Harvard I, I recall being impressed with the responsibility I was given in writing the purchase request for 400 engines, the biggest expenditure on such to date, being very careful in defining the engine configuration, its accessory drives, etc., going over this with the boss, John W. Young, and the Chief Engineer."

On September 28, 1938, Louis Wait flew the first Harvard I, N7000, under the watchful eyes of the British representatives responsible for overseeing Harvard and Lockheed Hudson production: Mr. H.C.B. Thomas of the Directorate of Technical Development, Sq Ldr James J. Addams, RAF, and Mr. H. C. Luttman, Aeronautical Inspection Directorate. Following successful completion of the test flights under Addams' supervision and shipment of N7000 on the MS Lochatrine October 24, Harvard production began on a large scale on the initial order of 200 aircraft.

In January 1939 the British Air Ministry ordered 200 more Harvards, which were to be shipped as previous machines, without engine and propeller, listed as additional equipment. Shipment to Liverpool was an involved process, with aircraft loaded at dockside in both Los Angeles and New York. The British assembly base was located at Shawbury while spares went to Hartlebury and Carlisle.

Luttman was assigned to NAA full time as the final British authority to approve shipment of airframes and spares. He was known as a quiet and most courteous, self-effacing gentleman who was a delight to work with. Addams and Thomas divided their time between Lockheed and North American. Thomas was responsible for approval of all materials and technical processes at both factories, while Addams, with 4,000 hours of flying time in more than 200 different aircraft, was official RAF test pilot at both companies. Later, when the RAF bought Douglas Bostons, these men were assigned to that company as well.

Addams was known as the opposite of Luttman since this RAF pilot with dashing moustache made it quite clear the Americans were mere Colonials who were to jump at his command. He cut quite a dashing figure among the Hollywood British set.

When Addams complained of inadequate cockpit heat, NAA said the problem would be solved if he could assign one of the completed Harvards to the company. Addams said absolutely not, he could not spare one, but he was certain the Air Corps would be happy to divert one of their aircraft for the tests. Addams ended up letting NAA have one and the familiar extended exhaust shroud over the right wing was developed, becoming a Harvard identification feature.

Those who saw it will not soon forget Addams' approach to the Inglewood airport in a Douglas Boston during those early days. Approaching from the east, he started to let down with the gear up. The NAA and Douglas flight ramp mechanics ran out, wildly waving, trying to wave him off. He looked out the open left side cockpit window, acknowledged the waving with a snappy salute, flared beautifully at gear down height, plopped onto the runway and slid to a halt. He climbed out, strode rapidly to a car and left without a word.

The Harvard rapidly found favor with British pilots and personnel. Mr. C. G. Grey, Editor, of the *THE AEROPLANE*, said that if the aircraft had the range to fly over Berlin, he was sure that all it would take to obtain a Nazi surrender would be to throw the prop into low pitch and run it up to max revs—the noise would do the rest.

Another 30 Harvard Is (NA-61) were built and

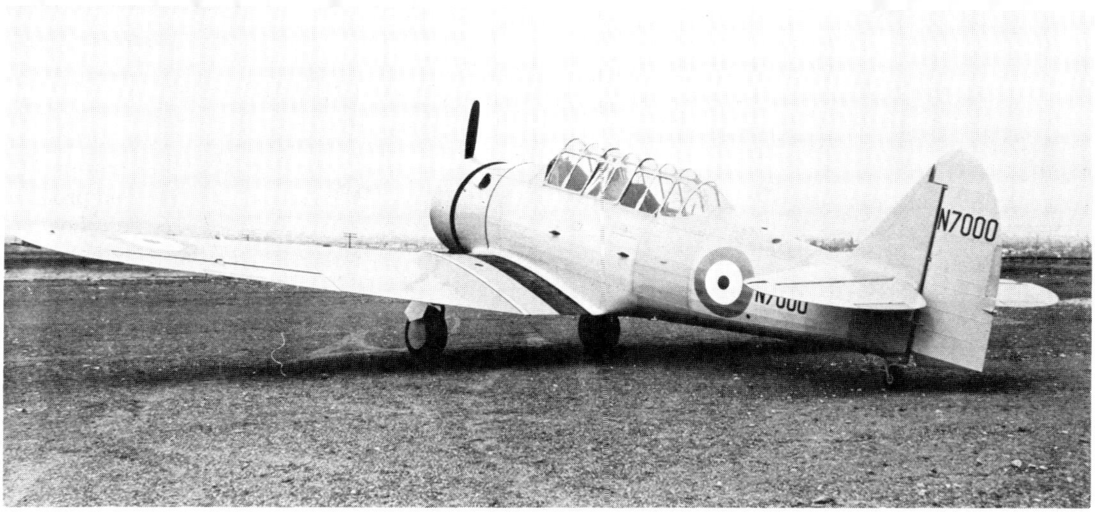

The first Harvard off the Inglewood production line, which flew for the first time on September 28, 1938. The aircraft was essentially a BC-1 with British-specified equipment. *(Dusty Carter/AAHS)*

From left to right, those most intimately connected with the Harvard, in front of the first aircraft: test pilot Paul Balfour, Ernest Breech, chief engineer Ray Rice, resident British tech officer H. C. B. Thomas, British inspector in charge H. C. Luttman, RAF Sqdn Ldr J. J. Addams, Dutch Kindelberger and Ken Rowan. *(Norm Avery)*

This is what Harvards looked like when they were taken cross country for assembly. Here the RAF 6th Motor Transport Company gets a convoy ready at the RAF base in Glasgow, Scotland, for transport to England on November 11, 1943. *(USAF)*

One of the early production Harvards in flight over England. *(via Pete Bowers)*

By 1938 the Air Corps BC-1s were getting in the public eye, as seen here at the National Air Races in Cleveland. *(Ralph Johnston via John Underwood)*

Based on the successful BC-1, the SNJ was ordered in September 1938 for use as a Navy scout trainer. This is the first SNJ-1, delivered to NAS Anacostia, Maryland, on May 29, 1939, being flown in July 1939 by an Anacostia test pilot. *(USN)*

The front cockpit of 1552 showing the overwater navigation chart board in place, another feature eliminated on later SNJs, but one that clearly showed the reason for calling the aircraft a scout trainer. *(USN)*

In all 177 BC-1s were ordered, with a great many going to National Guard and Reserve units. This line of BC-1s on August 6, 1938, heralded a new day in sophisticated training aircraft for the Army Air Corps. *(USAF)*

delivered to the RCAF, then Harvard production progressed through the remainder of the war as a part of the AT-6 production line.

The need for a modern scout trainer surfaced as a Navy requirement in 1938. Scouting, as it was then called, was an extremely important part of carrier aviation. Before the days of radar, the ability to scout far ahead of the force to seek out the enemy was a paramount mission in VSB squadrons. With monoplane scout bombers about to enter the USN inventory, a new trainer was required and a new instrument trainer was needed for Navy reserve squadrons.

BuAer did not have to look far—the Air Corps' successful BC-1 would fill the bill, as the British thought it would for them, and a detailed specification for the SNJ-1 (NA-52) was drawn up on September 29, 1938. Under Contract No. 62916 the Navy ordered 16 Scout Trainer North American (this is what SNJ stood for) aircraft. The first production SNJ-1, BuNo. (Bureau Number) 1552, was delivered to NAS Anacostia in Washington, D.C., on May 29, 1939, for flight testing. Before long it was obvious the Navy was quite happy with their new aircraft and a long chain of SNJs began.

The three BC-2s (NA-54) were trial aircraft to improve on the BC-1 featuring a three bladed propeller, all metal construction, squared wingtips, a triangular vertical stabilizer and some other improvements that included a few engine changes. Most of these features had already been tested on the NA-44, so there was not any innovation to speak of, but these changes brought a much improved version of the aircraft into the forefront. The three bladed prop did not prove to be that much of an improvement on the R-1340 so it was removed and the new aircraft was ordered as the BC-1A (NA-55) by the Army for the National Guard (29 aircraft) and the Air Corps Reserve (54 aircraft). For all intents and purposes, the aircraft would remain basically unchanged for the rest of its production life.

The last nine BC-1As were ordered under a new Advanced Trainer number and the AT-6 was born under the charge number NA-59—another 85 AT-6s were ordered and Louis Wait flew the first AT-6 on February 6, 1940. Wing span was 42 feet 7 inches, the same as the BC-1, but the square tips increased the wing area. The center section of one BC-1A was shortened by seven inches to become the BC-1B and before long the aircraft became standardized.

The Navy was quite pleased with the Air Corps product and ordered 61 aircraft as SNJ-2s, but it was not until the AT-6A and SNJ-3 (NA-77) that the aircraft became virtually identical with the revised center section (which, much to the dismay of the pilots who loved those long cross countries, cut the total fuel), triangular tail, R-1340-9 engine and removable fuel tanks. By this time the Dallas plant was open and, under charge number NA-78, AT-6As and SNJ-3s began to roll out with an NT behind their designations.

The third (38-450) of three BC-2s built to improve on the BC-1. Most of the features had been tested on the NA-44 and the aircraft quickly paved the way for an airframe that would remain basically unchanged throughout the life of the type. This BC-2 has a silver lacquer finish instead of the unpainted natural metal and it carries the Wright Field testing symbol. *(Pete Bowers)*

By early 1939 the venerable NA-16 was firmly established as a major military aircraft in several different countries. North American had founded its reputation on this one single type and, in large part due to the quality of the product, the basis of faith was laid for orders of other military aircraft. North American had earned its spurs, which would soon be riding herd on the B-25 Mitchell and the P-51 Mustang.

Vultee's BC-3 was an attempt to gain some of North American's lucrative market—it was similar to the BT-13 but had retractable landing gear and an R-1340-45 installed. *(USAF)*

Out of the BC-2 came the much improved BC-1A for the National Guard and the Reserve. Here 39-854 runs up—note the headrest which later disappeared from the series. *(Roger Besecker)*

NAA developed a single seat fighter version of their trainer, powered by an 870 hp R-1820. Seven went to Peru as NA-50s while another six as NA-68s were ordered by Siam (Thailand). Due to hostile Japanese moves in Southeast Asia, the U.S. absorbed the aircraft as P-64s for advanced fighter transition. *(USAF)*

Chapter Two

Naval Aviators and J-Birds

When Naval Aviators gather, they invariably turn the conversation to airplanes and among the old timers to the SNJ. As far as can be determined, more Naval Aviators flew the SNJ in their flying careers than any other single type of airplane in the Navy inventory. The "J-Bird," as it was called by Navy pilots, was well liked by many, intensely disliked by others, especially those who spent many months of their lives as instructors in the rear seat.

The aircraft was a delight to fly and it enabled many fledgling Navy types to experience their first taste of what a real service airplane was like. The engine was one of the most reliable ever produced: the airframe was strong, requiring very little maintenance; its ability to perform acrobatic maneuvers was not too shabby and the plane was inherently stable in all flight axies. On the minus side, to those who flew it as a steady diet, who could ever forget the nearly intolerable noise level in the cockpit, the "great" visibility from the rear seat and, forever remember, the cockpit heater . . . or lack of one . . . that did anything but produce tepid air. Cold air seemed to move like a wind tunnel across the instructor's feet in the winter and two or three flights a day in discomfort did not exactly endear the J-Bird to those assigned to that punishment for a two year tour.

The cockpit abounded with various knobs and projections, which lurked here and there to become knuckle busters when one had to quickly react to the many emergency drills required of a student Naval Aviator. The J was an excellent trainer because it demanded undivided attention, especially during landing, where it suddenly became a real handful to the unwary. It had the characteristic of inspiring confidence in a young pilot's ability to master the machine while, on the other hand, it could humble even the most cocky pilot who suddenly thought he had a bear by the tail in a strong, gusty crosswind. The art of the ground loop was learned by legions of pilots who thought they had it made on landing, only to learn that their particular North American product had a mind of its own.

The one single item which endeared the J to the hearts of thousands of Naval Aviators, however, was that in the SNJ they experienced the thrill and exhilaration of their first landing on an aircraft carrier at sea. Being equipped to land on a carrier set the SNJ series apart from all other AT-6 and Harvard aircraft.

The SNJ was available when the need arose for the Navy to greatly increase its training requirements from peacetime to wartime at the onset of World War II and North American Aviation was more than able to meet the challenge of producing airplanes at a rate necessary for the expansion period of the early 1940s. It was the Navy's ability to adapt the J for a variety of uses and the aircraft's adaptability to changing training requirements that enabled it to enjoy a long service life.

The Navy's long love affair with the SNJ, which enjoyed a production life of six years and a service life spanning two decades, goes back to 1936 when the Navy Bureau of Aeronautics wanted a monoplane with an enclosed cockpit that could be used for instrument training. Instrument flying was in its very early stages but its importance to the future of the Navy mission was recognized by military planners. It was obvious that the biplane era would soon draw to a close and a modern trainer with a cantilever wing design was necessary.

On December 14, 1936, the U.S. Navy ordered an improved version of the NAA BT-9 as the NJ-1 (NA-28) with 500 hp Pratt & Whitney R-1340-6 Wasp engines instead of the 400 hp Wright R-975. Most of the new production NJ-1s went straight to Pensacola, Florida, where they served as instrument trainers with VN5D8 at Corry Field. Three exceptions were BuNos. 0927, 0931 and 0947 which went to San Diego, California, and later Anacostia, Maryland, 0931 being attached to VB-3, a USS Saratoga squadron.

The NJ-1s presented a rather sleek, modern appearance in those days in contrast to the biplanes of an earlier era. They could even be described as gorgeous by those who flew them, resplendent in their colorful pre-war silver Navy trainer paint schemes with bright red cowls and red fuselage and wing bands. Squadron 5 even had some NJs painted similar to fleet airplanes with white cowls and bands and others with half red and half silver cowls.

A beautiful sight they were while pioneering the Navy's new training methods which were to be put to good use later. The NJs demanded the greatest respect during landing, especially the crosswind variety. The bird proved useful to the Navy for many years but the breed did not actively serve through the end of the war. The NJs, starting in late 1943 and ending July 1944, were ferried to the Navy technical training centers where they were stricken to serve as instructional airframes. The short career of the NJ-1 introduced the monoplane era to Navy training command.

By 1938 BuAer met its scout bomber training and instrument training requirement by ordering a Navy version of the BC-1. The first production SNJ-1 went to NAS Anacostia on May 29, 1939, for extensive tests after it had been demonstrated to the Inspector of Naval Aircraft at Inglewood, California. The report of this demonstration, as forwarded to BuAer, was satisfactory overall with the exclusion of spin tests which were not completed because the engine cut out in right hand spins.

In order to keep the program on schedule, it was recommended that this problem be resolved at Anacostia, which explains why so many different carburetors were tried on the aircraft during the tests. BuNo. 1552, as delivered, was powered by a P&W R-1340-06 engine of 500 hp with an NAY8C6M carburetor. Navy Board of Inspection and Survey (BIS) trials were conducted at the Navy flight test center, Anacostia, May 30 through December 4, 1939.

The trial board was under the chairmanship of Lcdr M.E.A. Gouin, USN, head of the test center. Later he was relieved as head of the board by Cdr "Just Plain George" Henderson, USN, who at the time was attached to the Bureau of Aeronautics. Naval Aviator 909, Henderson was a spark plug naval officer, who later went on to become executive officer of the USS Hornet, commander of the USS Princeton, commander of Task Force 77 during the Korean War, eventually to retire as a vice admiral. The rest of the board consisted of Lts W. K. Goodney, USN; S. A. Johnson, USN; R. E. Dixon, USN; L. P. Carver, USN; C. E. Giese, USN; Capt. William Saunders, USMC and Mr. E. W. Rounds.

The board lost no time in proceeding with tests.

NJ-1 BuNo. 0910 taxis down the flight line at Chevalier Field, Pensacola, Florida, in 1940. The sleek monoplane was a stark contrast to the biplanes in the background. *(Harry Gann)*

An SNJ-1 awaits its crew on the VN5D8 Squadron flight line at Corry Field, Pensacola, in the fall of 1939. The center section skid, to lessen the possibility of fire during a gear up landing, is visible under the fuselage. *(Bill Scarborough)*

An antispin chute was installed on June 2 and various carburetors were tested between June 3 and 20 before the engine cut-out problem was resolved with an NJ-1 NAY8J carburetor. On June 22 BuNo. 1552 was flown to Dahlgren, Virginia, for a contractor's demonstration. As delivered, the SNJ was not equipped with all items ordered on the production model, resulting in the pilot's chart board, blind flying hood and the CO_2 system being installed as the tests progressed.

On July 22, BuNo. 1552 returned to flight status after a 20 hour check. Up to this point the pilots were enthusiastic about the performance of the plane in spite of many problems which showed up in the first 20 hours. The engine was changed and the propeller was re-indexed a number of times to seek optimum performance. By mid-July, considerable trouble was experienced with the brakes. It was noted that the brakes had a nasty habit of grabbing and tightening on take-off, which the board attributed to expansion from the July heat. This necessitated frequent wheel removal, brake bleeding and brake clearance readjustment.

The engine began developing a history of high oil consumption, which continued for a number of reasons through the end of the test period. On July 25 the aircraft was subjected to the water hose test to determine the water tightness of the cockpit area, which turned out to be a horror story, as a close fitting canopy is not one of the ole J-Bird's attributes.

By early August enough flight time had accumulated for the trial board to recommend changes to the airframe and on August 22 the aircraft was flown back to Inglewood for installation of a globe valve in the hydraulic system and a spring loaded slip joint control rod to aid in the emergency extension of the landing gear. In addition a larger rudder tab was installed, a vent installed for the CO_2 system and Army type fuses were replaced with Navy items—at a unit price increase of $84.00 no less. Guess those Army fuses just weren't going to work in a Navy plane no matter what.

In addition, an attempt was made to eliminate flexing and vibration of the forward sliding cockpit enclosure when half open and to generally improve the water tightness of the cockpit enclosure, the cowling forward of the windshield, the baggage compartment and the cowling over the parachute flare compartment. While in California, 1552 flew numerous stability and rudder tab tests at both Los Angeles and San Diego, finally returning to Anacostia on November 7.

An SNJ-1 instrument trainer of VN5D8 after the addition of red band instrument training markings in 1940. Note that the radio antenna mast was located in the center of the cowling ahead of the windshield, as was the case in both the SNJ-1 and -2. Later it was offset to the right. *(USN)*

Oil consumption problems continued. On November 16, during an engine test, the engine consumed two gallons of oil in one hour and 40 minutes. Oil was seen leaking from the hydraulic pump drain. Packing was replaced but excessive oil consumption continued. On November 24, with Capt Saunders at the controls, the aircraft's engine consumed 2½ gallons of oil in 1½ hours. This alarmed the board and further attempts were made to determine the cause. Packing was replaced in the hydraulic pump and a new plug was manufactured for the end of the tower shaft. Although oil consumption remained high, it finally dropped somewhat so the tests could be completed.

During the last few days of the BIS trials, Lt Dixon* flew the final test on the emergency extension of the landing gear and Capt Saunders flew the final stability tests. All were satisfactory and on December 4, 1939, after a 20 hour check, the BIS trials came to an end with a total of 79 flights and 104.1 hours flying time. A new trainer had been evaluated by the Navy. Surely, as Capt Saunders stepped from the cockpit the last time on December 1, he had no idea that this aircraft was the first of many thousands that would serve the Navy well for the next 20 years.

The board was enthusiastic over the performance of the silver monoplane from Inglewood, which met its guaranteed design top speed of 205 mph at 4,755 pounds weight at rated altitude. Its service ceiling was confirmed to be 24,000 feet with a maximum rate of climb of 1,200 ft/min at 3,500 feet. Recommendations were made to modify the integral wing tank fuel system so that fuel flow in steep turns would be assured when fuel level in the tanks reached reserve capacity.

BuNo. 1552 remained at Anacostia for further evaluation until September 9, 1941, when it was transferred to Pensacola to replace BuNo. 1557 which had been destroyed in a crash on July 3. The SNJ-1s served faithfully into the early days

The first SNJ-2, BuNo. 2008, over Anacostia on May 7, 1940, during its test program. *(USN)*

The front cockpit of 2008. The pilot's chartboard is in the stowed position on the right side. *(USN)*

The unique instrument training hood over the front cockpit of 2008. It was fleet practice, however, to conduct instrument training using the rear hood and this feature disappeared later. *(USN)*

of World War II but as newer SNJs entered Navy service, the dissimilarity of types forced the Navy to make a hard decision. Standardization was important in a training environment and the SNJ-1 was just too dissimilar from later models.

*Robert E. Dixon would later become famous as commander of the USS Lexington's SBD Dauntless scout bombers in the Battle of the Coral Sea, May 7-8, 1942. He scored a direct hit, one of many, on the flight deck of the Japanese carrier Shoho. When the carrier sank, Cdr Dixon made his famous report, "Scratch one flattop." He would later retire as a Rear Admiral.

In late 1943 the decision was made to scrap the SNJ-1s and this version suffered the same fate as the NJ-1, BT-14 and other pre-war types that could not be adapted to the standardized scheme of things. None of the SNJ-1s survived the war in flying status. BuNo. 1552 was ferried to NATT Jacksonville, Florida, in November 1943 and was stricken on January 7, 1944. BuNos. 1554, 1555, 1558, 1560, 1564, 1565 and 1566 were all stricken at Jacksonville the same day. BuNo. 1556 lasted until July 31, 1944, when it was stricken at NAS Glenview, Illinois. The two SNJ-1s which lasted the longest were BuNos. 1559

SNJ-2 BuNo. 2566 of the second production batch in use as a station ready plane at NAS Jacksonville, Florida, on 18 April 1945. Most of the second run of -2s served as instrument trainers at Pensacola early in their service lives. *(USN)*

The Naval Reserve flew new SNJ-2s prior to World War II. BuNo. 2025 of NRAB Oakland, California, on the line in 1940. *(Balogh via Menard/Bowers)*

The first SNJ-3, BuNo. 6755, prepared for tests at the Naval Air Test Center, NAS Anacostia in Washington, D.C., April 1941. The -3 was the first of the J-Birds to be ordered in large quantities. *(USN)*

and 1561 which were assigned to the Marines at MCAS Quantico, Virginia. 1561 was stricken there on November 20, 1944, and 1559 was the last to go when scrapped at NAS Norfolk, Virginia, on November 30.

As work was progressing on the testing and delivery of the SNJ-1, Navy planners again looked to North American for follow-on aircraft to the SNJ-1 which would be used by the Reserve squadrons as an instrument and scout trainer. Detail specifications (SD-264-2a) were drawn up by the Navy on March 7, 1940, followed by an order for 36 airplanes based on the SNJ-1.

On the SNJ-2 (NA-65) the oil cooler was moved to the lower portion of the engine accessory section instead of the upper right venting out a scoop on the upper left accessory cowling. The carburetor intake was relocated to the left side of the engine, instead of underneath, and the cowling was redesigned into the familiar shape that would be used on all succeeding SNJ series. In essence, several of the improvements that turned the BC-1 into the AT-6 were incorporated into the Navy's product, with the odd exception of the original rounded rudder which did have an enlarged trim tab. The pilot's chartboard was retained, hinge mounted on the right side of the cockpit and folding up out of the way to latch to the glare shield. The fancy leather headrest of the SNJ-1 was retained but the instrument panels were updated.

The -2 retained the large 190 gallon integral wing tanks and external sump system as in the -1, but these were to prove troublesome when subjected to hard service use. The rectangular baggage door and large baggage compartment also was retained in the -2 as well as the radio homing antenna which was installed behind the rear seat.

Under contract No. 68924 the first flight of SNJ-2 BuNo. 2008 took place at Inglewood on March 29, 1940, with contractor demonstrations completed by April 5. The trainer, as delivered to Anacostia April 11, 1940, was powered by the 600 hp P&W R-1340-36. The empty weight was well within contractor guarantees at 3,773 pounds with full load weight being 4,978 pounds. BIS trials, once again under senior member Cdr George Henderson and the same personnel who conducted the SNJ-1 tests, began immediately. The plane flew 20 hours of testing between April 12 and April 30. Brake problems similar to those on the -1 became evident, requiring frequent wheel removal and brake adjustments. Leaks in the integral fuel tanks caused a halt to the testing twice while the tanks were drained and resealed. Both wings were removed during the 20 hour check to allow a thorough gas tank inspection. Top speed tests resulted in 214 mph at rated power at 6,000 feet with a service ceiling in excess of 24,600 feet. Tests were completed satisfactorily on May 14, 1940, after 26 flights and 38.6 hours flying time.

The board was very enthusiastic over the performance of the SNJ-2, highly recommending the plane for service use as, once again, a scout trainer. It is interesting to note that this airplane, possessing considerable range and speed comparable with service types of the day, resulted in the Bureau of Aeronautics often referring to the aircraft in writing as a possible service type scout, rather than a scout trainer landplane.

The board recommended improvement in the brakes and fuel tanks, that the prop governor control mechanism be redesigned and that an instrument flying hood be installed in the rear cockpit. Prior to this time, it was planned that all instrument training be conducted in the front seat with an instructor and lookout in the rear seat. Again they wanted the watertightness of the cockpit to be improved and the engine cowling modified to prevent cracking.

As a result of changes recommended by the trial board, the total cost for 36 aircraft went from $570,339.60 to $577,238.36 or $16,034.39 each.

As the Naval Reserves were in desperate need of a modern trainer, and were not assigned SNJ-1s, almost all of the initial batch of SNJ-2s went to them in 1940. BuNo. 2008 was retained at Anacostia as was BuNo. 2010. Recipients of other -2s were Naval Reserve Aviation Bases (NRAB) Miami, Detroit, Minneapolis, St. Louis, Kansas City, Long Beach, Chicago, Oakland, Seattle, Boston, New York, Anacostia and Philadelphia. A number of -2s were also delivered for station operations duties at NAS Norfolk, San Diego, Seattle, Miami and Quantico.

Two of the more interesting assignments were BuNo. 2012 which went to BAT-4, Pearl Harbor, and BuNo. 2018 to the U.S. Naval Attaché Buenos Aires. BuNo. 2018 served most of its service life in Argentina and was stricken there on December 31, 1945.

Meanwhile, as production of the SNJ-2 began, Navy training requirements dictated that more training aircraft were needed quickly. Inasmuch as the contract for the original order was already being filled, a new contract was necessary and detail specifications SD-264-2a were revised and submitted. Twenty-five more SNJ-2s (NA-79) were ordered under change 7 of Army Air Corps contract AC-12969. Navy regulations stated that with a new buy of airplanes, even with basically identical examples such as these, Production Inspection Trials be carried out. On November 25,

1940, BuAer, under Requisition Aero-1202-BU 40 ordered that it be done.

The first of the second production batch of SNJ-2s was BuNo. 2548 which was accepted by the Navy at Inglewood on December 20, 1940, and delivered for production testing at Anacostia on January 5, 1941. The board once again was under the able leadership of Cdr George Henderson who was assisted by the same group from the earlier two SNJ tests. 2548's trials were finished quickly as, according to the board comments, "this airplane is identical to the plane previously tested under contract No. 68924 and tests considered necessary are very brief." In addition, contract guarantees were not involved in the tests. The maximum speed tests did reveal 209 mph and 25,000 foot service ceiling which were very close to those obtained with BuNo. 2008. For the first time, the brakes did not cause a problem.

The SNJ-2 proved its worth and served the Navy well to the end of World War II. With its much larger fuel capacity than later series Js, the -2 was particularly popular with Naval Air Stations as a ready plane, weather ship and general purpose cross country training airplane.

As war clouds stormed over Europe in 1941, the Navy was faced with the immense problem of expanding flight training rapidly. Under the terms of BuAer Requisition 1255 and Army Air Corps contract AC-15977, both services combined their orders for the North American trainer—517 AT-6As and 120 SNJ-3s (NA-77) would be built at Inglewood while 1,330 AT-6As and 150 SNJ-3s (NA-78) would be built in the new NAA plant at Dallas, Texas, under an NT suffix. The Air Corps, according to the contract, would inspect and accept both Army and Navy versions. Since the Navy aircraft were being procured under an Army contract, guarantees would not be involved in testing the first aircraft.

The first SNJ-3, BuNo. 6755, was accepted by the Army for the Navy at Inglewood on March 7, 1941, and arrived at Anacostia for testing shortly thereafter. The -3 differed greatly from the -2, the major differences being the shorter wingspan (down to 42 feet 2 inches) caused by the use of a shorter center section and two separate 55.2 gallon fuel tanks which could be removed. The fuel selector was now internally mounted, front and rear instrument panels were revised, an instrument hood could be fitted over the rear seat, and the rear cockpit canopy hood was redesigned to fold forward with opening of the rear sliding hatch. Provisions were included for a forward firing .30 caliber machine gun in the upper cowl area and a .30 caliber swivel gun in the rear fuselage. The rear seat could be swiveled to the rear and the baggage compartment area was reduced, resulting in a smaller baggage door. A P&W R-1340-9 600 hp engine was installed and a triangular rudder was finally incorporated conforming to NA-44 standards. A steerable tailwheel was also incorporated, which would eventually draw criticism from the trial board and service units.

To add to the utility of the aircraft, it was equipped with provisions for the vertical mounting of an aerial camera in the rear fuselage section behind the seat. Camera bay doors were provided under the rear fuselage with viewfinder provisions under the rear seat. The combination of forward and rear firing armament, an oxygen system and camera provisions made the J-Bird the most versatile trainer the Navy employed up to that time.

The Anacostia test pilots were once again involved in the production trials and the BIS trials proceeded smoothly and quickly as the urgency of an impending war added considerable emphasis to the project. The empty weight of the test airplane was 4,075 pounds with gross weight set at 5,195 pounds. The maximum power test at 6,000 feet revealed a respectable 206.5 mph and a service ceiling somewhat less than the SNJ-1 and -2 at 23,500 feet.

Interestingly enough, certain problems were encountered with the -3 that were not apparent in the previous two models. Some of these may have resulted from the redesign of the smaller center section and rudder and possible small changes in the wing and tail incidence angles. The board complained of poor lateral stability in the landing configuration, especially near the stall, and that directional stability at small angles of yaw was poor. Considerable difficulty was experienced with the packing in the main landing gear oleo struts. Both split and solid type packing rings were tried during the next test phase with a combination of the two finally settled upon to resolve the leak problem.

At this point the board no longer made an issue out of the lack of cockpit watertight integrity—a major redesign of the cockpit canopy structure would have resulted in production delays, so the North American product would forever rattle, roar and leak. When the testing was complete, the board listed a considerable number of recommended modifications to the airplane: directional stability at small angles of yaw should be improved, lateral stability in the landing configuration at speeds near the stall were less positive than desirable, satisfactory oleo struts should be provided for the landing gear, a wrench should be designed and provided for

SNJ-3 BuNo. 6775 of VN3D8 carries the classic instrument training high visibility red markings in the summer of 1942. *(USN)*

servicing the shock struts, increase the effectiveness of the rudder tab, provide a lockable instead of a steerable tailwheel, provide aileron trim tabs controllable from the pilot's cockpit. This last point is interesting in that the feature was also recommended on the -4 and -5 series as well as a "DC" meaning "Desirable—Contractor's Responsibility." NAA obviously felt that the cost involved in the design and installation of this item in both Army and Navy versions was not warranted since it was never done, which is surprising with an aircraft of this size, horsepower and weight.

New production SNJ-3s went straight to the Navy's rapidly expanding training complexes in Miami, Pensacola and Jacksonville. Many of the early -3s went to Squadrons 3 and 5 at Corry and Chevalier Field, Florida. Those used for instrument training bore the most colorful of all the paint schemes applied to J-Birds with natural metal fuselages, two color wings with yellow above and silver below, red cowls, red tails and red instrument trainer bands on wings and fuselage. They did not last long with the outbreak of war when fancy and impractical paint jobs became unnecessary. Although many SNJs would still be delivered later in the war with the inboard portion of the wing panels painted yellow, the planes never equalled the glamor of the pre-war era.

As 1941 progressed, the American armed forces hurried into an expanding training program. Both the Army and the Navy realized the AT-6/SNJ series was the best aircraft to standardize on, being far more reliable, easier to fly, more versatile and not encumbered with troublesome landing gear and brake systems which had plagued the Curtiss SNC. The Pratt & Whitney R-1340 had already proved itself to be extremely durable and reliable with standardization on the AN-1 variant.

On April 10 1941, the Army and the Navy placed an order for 2,970 AT-6Cs and 2,400 SNJ-4s (NA-88) to be built in Dallas under Army Air Corps Contract W535 AC-19192. The SNJ-4, as stated in the contract specifications, was generally similar to the SNJ-3 with the addition of bomb rack provisions in the wings, space for a .30 caliber gun in the right wing and a gun camera in the left wing.

The first SNJ-4, BuNo 05527, was delivered to NAS Anacostia for Production Trials on June 7, 1942. The plane actually arrived earlier than anticipated and the paperwork to commence flight testing was back dated to get the program started. The trial board met on June 9 and testing proceeded quickly on the first SNJ variant to have two forward firing guns. Wooden footrests were installed which the test pilots later found to be somewhat weak. Since the aircraft was basically similar to the -3, flight testing was wrapped up by the middle of July. In the trial board's report to BuAer, dated July 20, 1942, only minor problems or modifications were noted. An automatic carburetor and cockpit controlled aileron trim were again recommended along with strengthened wooden foot rests in the cockpit and relocation of the right instrument panel light which interfered with the operation of the gun charging handle.

An SNJ-3 being readied for flight, summer 1942, at Chevalier Field, Pensacola. *(Nav Air History)*

Curtiss SNC-1 Falcons and SNJ-3s share the instrument training line at NAS Miami, Florida, in June 1942. Due to continuing problems, the SNC never became a major advanced trainer in the Navy. *(USN/National Archives)*

The cluttered flight line at NAS Jacksonville in Late 1942 illustrates the rapid build-up of the Naval Air Training Command after the onset of World War II. Obsolete types such as the BT-1 helped fill the gap in training until SNJ production reached its peak. *(USN/National Archives)*

An SNJ-3 used at the Naval Photographic Training Center, Chevalier Field in the summer of 1943. The photographer is using a Fairchild F-56 hand held aerial camera. SNJ-3 photo trainers were painted in light gull grey with yellow wing tips and cowling leading edges. *(USN)*

The first production SNJ-4, BuNo. 05527, during the BIS (Board of Inspection and Survey) trails at the Naval Air Test Center, Anacostia, on July 1, 1942. This was the first of the SNJs delivered for testing with forward firing guns installed. *(USN)*

The Dallas production line full of SNJ-4s on July 15, 1942. Full scale production of the -4 was underway as testing of the prototype -4 continued at Anacostia. *(Dusty Carter/ AAHS)*

Many of the new SNJ-4s stayed right in the state of Texas for their first service tour, going straight to the huge Corpus Christi complex, which would eventually include the satellite fields of Rodd, Cabiness, Waldron, Cuddihy, Kingsville and Beeville. Although all of these air stations received SNJs in varying quantities, the major SNJ units with 100 to 150 aircraft each were Squadrons 14A and 14C, both VF (fighter) at Kingsville; Squadron 14B (VF) at Corpus Main Base; Squadrons 15A and 15B, both VA (dive bombing) at Kingsville, and Squadrons 16A and 16B, both VT (torpedo) at Waldron.

A brand new SNJ-4 on its Navy acceptance flight near the NAA plant at Dallas, Texas. The aircraft is being flown by a U.S. Army Air Corps pilot—since SNJs were bought under AAF contracts and the plant was under Army jurisdiction, Army pilots accepted Navy aircraft at the factory during World War II. *(Harry Gann)*

As World War II progressed the shortage of gasoline, rubber, brass and aluminum became of major importance. The War Department issued an order to conserve strategic materials, particularly in training aircraft, where possible. Vultee and North American were directed to develop wooden substitute structures wherever feasible for the SNV and SNJ. The manufacturers complied quickly and many of the early SNJ-4s and AT-6Cs were delivered with wooden control sticks, foot rests, baggage compartment floors and trim tabs. As soon as capable subcontractors could be found to produce the rear fuselage monocoque and horizontal stabilizers from wood, these were incorporated in production at Dallas. There were 270 SNJ-4s, BuNo. 26869-27138, and 181 AT-6Cs, Serial Nos. 41-33068 to 41-33072 and 42-3884 to 42-4063, produced with wood stabilizers while 1,040 SNJ-4s BuNos. 27139-27851 and BuNos. 51350-51676, and 1,043 AT-6Cs, Serial Nos. 42-4064 to 42-4243, 42-48772 to 42-49069, 42-43847 to 42-44411, had both wood stabilizers and wood fuselage monocoques.

The wood fuselage was constructed of three-ply mahogany plywood used on the outskin skin covering, bulkheads and shear webs. Longerons, stringers, stiffeners and bulkhead flanges were made of solid spruce. Maply comprewood was spliced to the spruce members where extra loads were expected to be absorbed. In some locations 24ST aluminum alloy was used to reinforce fittings. The skin panels were scarf-spliced and grain direction was set at 45 degrees to vertical frames and bulkheads. Various wood substitutions were used, depending upon the vendor.

The wooden construction was extremely strong although durability suffered in humid climates as the units aged in service. The wooden stabilizers were of similar construction with the addition of spruce stiffeners, spar caps and maple elevator hinge support blocks.

Total aluminum saved with wood trim tabs, floor trays, sticks, seats, rear fuselage and stabilizers came to 200 pounds per aircraft or 420,000 pounds for 2,100 Army and Navy aircraft. The wood versions were actually heavier since wood outweighs aluminum but the experiment was tried. Pilots often remarked the wooden aircraft were lighter on the controls than their aluminum brothers—in reality they were heavier but psychology and preconceptions are hard to overcome.

The SNJ-4 was the most numerous of the series, with a few serving into the late 1950s when the Js were phased out. Fifty-one SNJ-4s were passed to the French Navy in 1952, serving with various Aeronavale units in Morocco. After 1961 most of the remaining French SNJs were ceded to the Moroccans, a few still serving Aeronavale units in France until 1971.

The SNJ-5/AT-6D was essentially a follow-on program under the same Army Air Forces contract but the electrical system was switched from 12 to 24 volts. The Navy received 1,357 SNJ-5s while the Army got 2,604 AT-6Ds and another 800 AT-6Ds as NA-121s.

By October 5, 1943, one of the early production SNJ-5s, BuNo. 51847, was delivered to the Navy's new test center at Patuxent River, Maryland, where the USN was expanding its testing programs and coordinating all test functions under one command. No problems were encountered in the production trials which lasted until

November 20, 1943. Tests were conducted at a gross weight of 5,250.8 pounds with the only substantive recommendation being, once again, the addition of aileron tab control from the cockpit.

This bird was then passed to the radio and electrical test section which completed test work on December 20. Only minor problems were encountered and 51847 passed on to the Armament Test section where a most complete test on the SNJ armament system was carried out. Since the aircraft was delivered without armament, considerable delay was encountered in obtaining the necessary parts. Almost five weeks elapsed before the necessary parts were installed.

The initial installation was completed on March 27, 1944, with air tests starting on March 30. The bomb racks became a concern when it took two men more than 60 man-hours to install the bomb racks, cables and release handle. Each bomb rack had five stations which gave the plane a total capacity of ten M-41 20-pound or ten M-5 30-pound fragmentation and bombs. Four 100 pound shackles could be mounted over stations two and four of the R-1502 rack which provided the following bomb loading combinations: a) six fragmentation and two 100-pound bombs, b) ten 20-pound or 30-pound fragmentation bombs, c) two fragmentation or four 100-pound bombs, d) four 100-pound bombs.

Release tests revealed that the 100-pound bomb had a tendency to hang up on the suspension hook. Air tests of the bomb rack started on April 6, 1944, and nearly resulted in disaster. The test pilot entered a standard 60° dive bombing run at 4,000 feet and at 2,000 feet was gingerly trying to recover from an incredible (for the J-Bird) dive speed of 280 mph. This was considerably beyond the 250 mph maximum safe speed established for the airplane and the pilot was fearful of imminent structural failure during recovery. Needless to say, after that no further dive tests were attempted. In addition, it was recommended that the SNJ not be used as a dive bombing trainer.

The tests with the forward firing .30 caliber Browning machine guns went well, however, and a total of 4,075 rounds was fired from the cowl gun with only two stoppages. The wing gun managed 4,125 rounds with only six stoppages. The rearward firing swivel mounted gun fired 4,135 rounds with eight total stoppages. Problems were encountered with the free gun link collector, causing interference with the gun mount.

Production Trials on the SNJ-5 were completed on May 26, 1944—oddly enough, it took longer to test the -5 and complete the paperwork (finally signed on June 21) than any of the other SNJ series. Everything was noted as satisfactory with the exception of dive bombing. The board also noted that flight characteristics were little changed due to the control system modification which changed the control movement limits from late SNJ-4s and AT-6C-15s on. In the earlier aircraft, the aileron travel was 30° up and 15° down which was changed to 15° up and 15° down to reduce the possibility of aileron structural failure at full throw near maximum airspeed. The rudder travel was changed from 35° to 30°.

During the production life of the AT-6D/SNJ-5, 900 airframes were built with wooden fuselage monocoques and wood stabilizers which broke down into 440 AT-6Ds, 276-SNJ-5s* and 284 British Harvard Mk IIs. The most complex of the wooden substructures was the rear fuselage, built by Kroehler-Koak Co., Berkey & Gay Co. and, of all people, the H. J. Heinz Co. who became famous for their 57 varieties of canned food. Many of these -5s would later receive metal structures to replace the wood as the war ground to a halt.** In addition, SNJ-4s and -5s would have their tailwheels modified to lockable/steerable after the war.

To further fulfill its training needs after production phaseout of the SNJ-5, the Navy purchased 411 SNJ-6s (NA-121) by taking over that many AT-6Fs from the U.S. Army Air Force. The -6 differed from the -5 in that the rear seat swivel gun was eliminated, the wing gun and camera were removed, bomb racks were removed, a full vision rear hood replaced the gunner's hood, vertical camera provisions were deleted, and a rectangular baggage door and enlarged baggage compartment, as last used on the SNJ-2, was provided. The -6 and the AT-6F also contained provisions for an auxiliary 20 gallon centerline drop tank. Although earlier models of the AT-6/SNJ had been considered for a small internal auxiliary fuel tank under the baggage compartment for ferry purposes, the -6 was the only production model that was fitted with auxiliary fuel provisions. The cowl gun was the only armament provision retained and the -6 had strengthened outer wing panels to increase wing service life as well as the latest instrumentation and radio equipment. A lockable tailwheel would later be retrofitted to this version.

---

*BuNos. 43638-43850, 44031-44037, 52047-52049, 84819-81871.

**Coauthor Ohlrich's personal SNJ-5, BuNo. 43689, was one such aircraft.

As the drama of World War II unfolded, Naval Aviation became enmeshed in the greatest expansion program ever experienced before or since that time. When the Japanese attacked Pearl Harbor on December 7, 1941, the Navy had on hand 6,000 Naval Aviators, of whom 4,000 were combat pilots . . . there was an immediate need for 30,000 within a year. Even though appropriations were available, an air arm could not appear overnight. No large scale aviation training programs were in existence in any of the military services.

The professionally staffed training units at Pensacola basically taught pilots how to fly an airplane, with the advanced training undertaken by the fleet units themselves. Clearly, changes had to be made as the fleet needed combat-ready trained pilots on a grand scale. Consequently, all flight training of USN pilots in World War II was relegated to shore commands. The Navy tried to maintain its high standard of pilot training by adhering to a basic philosophy: a) quality first, quantity second; b) technical superiority; c) emphasis on Navy training as well as flight training; d) teamwork among all branches of the Naval service.

As a result, Naval flight training in World War II consisted of: 1) Preflight/25 weeks; 2) Primary/15 weeks; 3) Intermediate/22 weeks; 4) Operational—10 weeks (these figures changed somewhat as the war progressed). Initially, four colleges were designated for Preflight training: University of North Carolina, U of Georgia, U of Iowa and St. Marys of California. In addition, Primary flight schools sprang up at a score of Naval Air Stations all over the country such as Paso, Washington; Minneapolis; Cape Girardeau, Missouri; New Orleans; Dallas; Hutchinson, Kansas; Norman, Oklahoma, to name a few. Fortunately, America was blessed with a large number of experienced civilian pilots who provided the expertise necessary to train the needed pilots of all services.

The flight training program was altered as necessary during the war to adapt to changing conditions. At one point the Navy had too many students in the program so many were sent back to school, some to be recalled later. Industry proved up to the task of providing the planes to train the 30,000 new pilots per year. The Navy bought training aircraft of all types and as an interim, many obsolete operational types, such as BT-1s and OS2Us, were pressed into service as trainers. Those who came into the various Navy Cadet training programs (V-5, V-12, Civilian Pilot Training, etc.) well remember the various types of Navy equipment used in Primary training. Many soloed in NE-1s (Piper Cubs), Taylorcrafts, NP-1s (Spartans), N2T-1s (Timms), NR-1s (Ryans) as well as the more familiar Boeing Stearman N2S and Naval Aircraft Factory N3N "Yellow Peril" series of biplanes.

After Primary, most of the student Naval Aviators went to Intermediate at the Navy's "Academies of Aviation," the greatly expanded Pensacola, Florida, or Corpus Christi, Texas, complexes. Here, they would be introduced to the Vultee SNV for instruments and formation, then the SNJ for more instruments, formation, dive bombing, aerial gunnery, strafing and night flying. In addition, the Navy maintained an Aerial Photo School at Chevalier Field, Pensacola, which functioned there throughout the war and, in fact, until the closing of Chevalier. Extensive use was made of the SNJ in the photo training role with both hand held and vertically mounted cameras.

Instructors to train this mighty armada were never present in enough numbers until the end of the war. For the most part, the average instructor possessed considerable motivation and enough teaching ability and flying talent to produce an excellent product. Not all were gifted aviators, however, and many were not good Naval officers either.

Lt. Robert Schipf, USNR (Ret) recalled such a person while going through the program as an enlisted Student Naval Aviation Pilot. "In 1945 I was assigned a solo flight at Whiting one day and reported to the flight line for my SNJ. Shortly after leaving the ground, at an altitude of only some 30 or so feet, the plane began a strong roll to the left. I found that I could not control the aircraft and cut the throttle all the way back. The plane immediately righted itself and I landed on the remaining runway. On taxiing back to the line, I filled in the usual 'bitch' sheet and gave it to the chief on duty. He gave me a lot of lip, but I insisted that the controls be checked out. In the ready room, I was asked for an explanation of my aborted hop, this by the lieutenant in charge. I told my story and was called a loafer and everything else in the book. The next day, one of the instructors came over to me and asked the side number of the plane which gave me the trouble. I told him the number and he said, 'Darn it, that's the same plane I had this morning. It did the same thing and I was almost killed. Maybe they'll look at it now.' So far as I know, something was stuck in one of the aileron areas but I never again heard of the plane and was never given an explanation."

"One day at Memphis, I returned from a solo N2S flight and taxied to the line. I was placed in position by a lineman and battened down. Immediately, the truck came by and refueled the plane before I got away. As I started off I was asked to get back in to take it elsewhere. We cranked up again and off I went to a spot several hundred yards away. A new lineman took over and I again closed up shop. Again a truck came along to refuel. On finding a full tank, the driver reported to the chief instructor who immediately called me on the carpet. I was accused of taking off, landing as soon as possible in a close-by place, and loafing until the period was over. The officer condemed me unmercifully for days over this incident and I presume that it is duly recorded in my records to this day." These few bad apples in the barrel caused more than their share of heartache to those pressing on to earn their wings of gold. Luckily they were relatively few in number.

On the other hand, there were the dedicated men who kept the aircraft in good shape. A. A. Tegtmeier, Jr., was a rated Aviation Mechanic during World War II at Barin Field, Alabama, a part of the Pensacola complex, where he began as a Seaman First Class plane captain. "Surrounded by 450 SNJs," he recalled, "I was given a section leader's job. I had twelve Js and 12 plane captains to herd. After the guys had run the planes up each day, I would review their problems or queries and in checking the condition of the plane, I'd decide if it was to be grounded—due for a trouble shooter to come out and look at it—or have it sent to Engineering.

"The biggest gripe, I recall, was the plane just back from one of the periodic clock checks and too much grease coming off the prop housing and clouding the windshield. Or, the tailwheel didn't want to straighten or unstraighten. Several wheels up landings—crunch, and the pilot couldn't figure out what that loud noise was honking at him just before touching down.

"The infamous Vultee SNV Vibrator was aboard. I believe we had six or so which were used for towing targets for awhile. All kinds of crazy memories flood in—German prisoners of war from Africa cleaned up the base. A pregnant Wave hung herself with her radio cord—she was a radio mechanic striker and her boy friend refused to acknowledge himself as being the daddy. The battery was continually stolen from the fire truck. Wild machine gun rounds killed some cows at Gulf Shores. But the SNJ stands out—it truly was a fine advanced trainer fighter plane for its day."

By early 1943 the main Pensacola SNJ squadrons with at least 100 planes each were VN3D8—Instrument and Instructor School at Chevalier, VN4D8 (VF) Barin (westside), VN5D8 (VA) Bronson, VN6D8 (VT) Barin (eastside). At the same time VN1D8 at Ellyson and VN2D8 at Saufley were equipped with SNVs and VN9D8 at Corry had SNBs (Beech 18s for twin training). The main SNJ units toward the end of the war at Pensacola were the Instructors School at Chevalier, VN3D8 at South Whiting, VN4D8 at Barin, VN5D8 at Bronson and VN6D8 at Corry, all with the same syllabus.

The VF, VT, VA designations were later dropped. VN6D8 was decommissioned late in the war and the mass movement of Corry's SNJs to Saufley North and VN3D8A was an exciting event that is still remembered by the participants.

The pressures of war and the urgently accelerated pace of flight training during the period naturally produced some rather bizarre flying activities and a somewhat appalling accident rate. The events were not the fault of the airplanes but rather the circumstances. Many of the finer points of flying were simply overlooked or omitted because there wasn't enough time.

Cdr. Jack Hoey, USNR (Ret), who was an instructor at Pensacola during this time, summed up the situation with his own reflections. "In those days, the Navy was losing pilots in combat at an incredible rate—they needed pilots in the fleet desperately. The sense of urgency to get the students trained as quickly as possible and get them out to the fleet was evident at all levels of flying training, especially basic. This, coupled with rivalry of the various SNJ squadrons and the aggressiveness of the instructors, produced an incredible story."

It was about this time that NAAS Barin Field earned the nickname "Bloody Barin." The spirit at Barin was as high as anywhere. For awhile even the SNJs based there were painted in fleet colors of blue and white, but early in the war tragedy struck in a big way and 15 pilots were killed in a single month. No other SNJ training base ever topped this record. One of the pilots killed that month was the son of famed columnist Walter Winchell. Most of these crashes occurred because of mid-air collisions, flathatting, lack of air discipline, stall-spin or just stupid "Dilbert" mistakes. A Navy board of investigation was convened to look into the matter, but not much was really done except tighten up on air discipline.

Capt Mark O. Shriver, USNR (Ret) recalls standing in the Barin chow line and witnessing mid-air collisions in the traffic pattern. "There was virtually no traffic pattern to speak of in the daytime and what passed for one at night was usually scary. I remember routinely having nine SNJs on the runway at Barin at one time, having very near misses at night and getting shot at while towing targets for air-to-air gunnery (some people came back with bullet holes). The whole program at Barin, or at any of the other crowded bases, was hairy to say the least." The nickname has remained, even to the present among Pensocola based pilots.

To those who lived the aerial adventure of that era, hairy tales and tragedy were facts of life. Consider the instructor who led his five students off on a tactics and formation hop. Often, at the completion of a successful flight, the instructors would have the students slide into a tail chase formation, with each plane flying about one plane length behind and slightly below the one in front. The instructor this day looped and rolled his charges back to the vicinity of the field on top of a broken cloud layer. Remembering that the cloud base was about 1,800 feet, he split-Sed his flight down through a hole, only to find the cloud base was now 600 feet. The first four SNJs drilled into the ground quite close to each other. The remaining two pilots escaped with their lives, albeit with overstressed and somewhat wrinkled airplanes.

One must also consider the "Dilberts" of the day who added their share of problems to others, like the student from Whiting who entered the traffic pattern head-on to traffic and caused two others to crash while avoiding him. This turned out to be the same guy who later, while flying an N3N, decided to try the flare handle to see if it worked—it did and the flare landed in a bomb dump which caused mass hysteria for awhile among the ground troops.

A classic story came out of both the Army Air Force and the Navy, one ascribed to Kelly Field and the other to Corpus Christi—both in Texas. As cadets, or "Gadgets" as they were nicknamed, "cruised about the Texas plains after dark, they began harassing train crewmen to the point of serious injury. They would spot a slow freighter ambling along a track, fly ahead of it for several miles, turn and meet the locomotive in a low approach, and wait until they were right on the engine before turning on one landing light. The engineer would *know* that he could not stop in time to avoid a *sure* collision, and order the fireman to jump"* before the "other train" hit. The engineer promptly slammed on the brakes and ground the wheels flat as the SNJ or AT-6 roared overhead and the cadet hightailed it back to base with his night flying completed. No doubt both Army and Navy pilots took part in this exercise of skill, daring and stupidity as word got around after the first guy tried it.

Jack Hoey recalls missing a few odds and ends in the course of flight training while an instructor with VN6D8 at Corry (Jack was a more typical instructor of the day—one who loved to fly, especially in the SNJ, who gave his all as an instructor and flew every chance he could get). One accident was caused by, of all things, the marker beacon which was installed in some of the later SNJs . . . "No training at all was conducted in its use—it was simply ignored and was a mystery to most cadets and some instructors. When some cadets unknowingly went over a beacon and the amber light would blink, many yelled, 'Mayday.' One instructor, when he noted the blinking light, yelled, 'Mayday, my fuel is gone—I'm going in.' He proceeded to force land himself in an Alabama pasture where he hit a cow broadside."

Jack also relates a tale of courage that happened one day in 1943. "During the 'Fam' [familiarization] portion of training at VN6D8, we would take our student to a grass field called 'Helm's Tract.' It was very large and had two white circles at either end. After demonstrating the technique of landing in the circle, the instructor got out and the student had to hit the circle three times flying solo. This means we had four or five students in the pattern and a like number of instructors sitting on the grass observing. One of the instructors had just left the plane and his student pulled out and prepared to take off. He held his brakes and with full throttle was ready to roll, when another solo student came in over the trees behind him and did not see the plane on the ground. The landing SNJ hit the other plane with his main gear smashing the greenhouse—the force of impact broke off the left wheel of the take-off plane. The pilot was knocked unconscious. The airborne SNJ took a wave-off and returned to Corry. The left gear of the grounded SNJ was now only a stub—the wheel was gone.

"The pilot was unconscious and full throttle was on. The plane began to turn counterclockwise around the stub, driving it farther into the ground. The pilot was being banged around the cockpit further injuring him and no matter what he did, there was no stopping the situation as long as full throttle was on. We tried running with the wing to jump up to the cockpit, but if you ran inside the turn, you had to run backwards. On the outside, it was too fast and the tail would cut you down, followed by that prop at full rpm. We tried grabbing the tail, but it knocked us back. Round and round that J-Bird went. Finally from out of the group of instructors came Lt(jg) Joe Fail from Tennessee. I looked around and he was doing what all country boys do in an emergency—he was taking off his shoes and getting down to his bare feet. He threw off his helmet (cloth), dropped his chute harness and took off for the outside edge of the wing. He

---

*Lt. William M. Bell as told to George A. Reynolds, MILITARY JOURNAL, Vol. 2, #3, Winter 1978/79, p. 9.

Undoubtedly the base which operated the most SNJs at any one time in World War II was the huge North and South Field complex at Kingsville, Texas. The field was commissioned on July 4, 1942, very shortly becoming the home of four large SNJ squadrons. Over 50 new SNJ-4s can be counted here on the line in the winter of 1942. *(USN/National Archives)*

Kingsville based SNJs practice formation flying in August 1942. At one time during the war, Kingsville had over 500 SNJs sprinkled among the four squadrons and base support aircraft. *(USN/National Archives)*

With the tow line attached to the right wing bomb rack, a Kingsville J picks up speed in November 1942 for a short field take-off to snatch an aerial gunnery target sleeve into the air, hopefully without tearing it. The target sleeve has been wrapped tight to give some stability as it gets airborne. *(USN/National Archives)*

Kingsville pilots look for the tell-tale colored holes which indicate the number of .30 caliber hits scored on the sleeve. By the dejected look on this bunch, they appear to be having trouble locating any holes this fine November 1942 day. *(USN/National Archives)*

ran in circles until his speed was equal to that wing tip, then like a jackrabbit, he leaped into the area of the circling wing and dove for the wing root where it meets the cockpit. His left hand barely caught the edge of the cockpit. He hung on, pulled himself up, reached over and cut the throttle. He was drunk for three days after."

There was several instances of the ole two place J being used to carry two additional passengers. On two of these occasions a couple of aviators flew from Colorado Springs to Boulder, Colorado, to pick up their "dates" and flew them back to Colorado Springs. One can only imagine tooling around up in those mountains in the evening with a girl on one's lap.

There were three distinct evolutions of basic training to which the SNJ was found particularly useful, other than basic formation, acrobatics, night flying and the other standard syllabus items. These were aerial photography, fixed aerial gunnery and carrier operations. Although not ideally suited for flexible gun training, the Navy did utilize the plane for teaching rear seat gunners on a limited scale. Initially, some Navy gunners were sent to Harlingen, Texas, where they trained in Army Air Force AT-6s utilizing the Matagorda firing range. The Navy found the SNJ rear gun operation rather troublesome and eventually shifted the bulk of this training to more suitable types such as the OS2U and SBD.

In the fixed firing role, training value was excellent, with the J used in this manner until it was retired. Although the cowl gun was never a precise weapon (it was never really meant to be), it provided the needed experience for fledgling combat pilots learning air-to-air and air-to-ground gunnery technique.

Capt Hec Davis, USN (Ret) recalled considerable time devoted to live gunnery with Squadron 14C at Kingsville, Texas, in early 1945. "After completing instrument training, I went to Kingsville (South Field) where the SNJs were used for advanced training. The course at this time consisted of formation, tactics (including air-to-air combat), aerial gunnery (firing at a towed sleeve over the Gulf), strafing (T-targets on Padre Island), navigation, more instruments and night flying with a total flight time of about 120 hours."

The target sleeves were towed aloft by an SNJ equipped with a tow hook and a release handle in the cockpit. On early series aircraft the tow hook was mounted behind the tail wheel. All later modifications utilzed a tow hook attached to the bomb rack release under the wing. The final arrangement consisted of a large cannister carried on the bomb rack under the right wing, with the sleeve being released and streamed into the air.

Making a tow take-off with the SNJ during the war was always an interesting proposition, as Jack Hoey remembered. "We would line up on the runway with the tow rope stretched out in front of the plane along the edge of the runway. The tow ring was then attached to the hook under the wing. We would use full flaps and full power to get airborne quickly so the sleeve wouldn't be dragged down the runway and destroyed before it got airborne. When we passed the sleeve on the takeoff roll, we would pull up steep so the sleeve would be lifted off without too much jerk. When we returned, we made a low pass and when a flagman dropped his flag, we pushed the release handle and hoped the sleeve would disengage and drop. However, it often did not release and I made many landings with the rope and sleeve still attached to my SNJ."

The Navy made little use of the wing gun for gunnery training, preferring the relatively simple and easy to maintain cowl gun. The gun sight was mounted on the cockpit floor and the sight image was projected up through a hole in the glare shield to the reflector glass. The gun camera was mounted in the left wing and when it worked, it worked well. The film would later be used to evaluate the students' faults; however, the Type W-7B wing cameras were so troublesome that some units did not make much use of them.

The cowl gun was manually charged by the pilot as the receiver of the gun protruded into the cockpit. There was a cutout in the upper right portion of the instrument panel for this purpose. The pilot merely pulled aft on the manual charging handle (as did the World War I aces) to slip a live round in the chamber for firing or to clear a jam. The spent cartridge cases and links were ejected into a chute which was later emptied via a small access door in the lower right side of the fuselage over the wing. The gun was equipped with a type E-4 gun synchronizing unit mounted on the rear engine case which permitted it to fire through the propeller arc. The unit worked well, considering the literally millions of rounds of ammunition that were fired by the SNJ during its service life.

Occasionally, however, the unit did malfunction and a bullet would fire through a prop blade, passing neatly through to leave a small hole on the rear face of the blade and a jagged edge on the front. Surprisingly, little vibration resulted but there was a distinct whistle audible on the ground when the plane returned to land. The prop would be removed, the hole would be dressed and smoothed and if the hole was not too near a blade edge, it would be balanced (sometimes by drilling a like hole in the other blade) and returned to service. Smoothing the hole would eliminate the whistle but not the apprehension of the pilot who was assigned one of the planes for more gunnery. The nagging thought was always there—what happens if the thing malfunctions again and puts *another* hole in same blade? Hope it doesn't happen this flight. In those units regularly using the SNJ for gunnery, it was not uncommon to see a few props on the line with holes in them.

The need for an adequate trainer for the teaching of carrier landings to future carrier pilots manifested itself early in the war. The only carrier training done up to that time was accomplished in fleet aircraft. The Navy hurriedly pressed obsolete types such as the BT or SB2U into training but it soon became obvious that a cheap, relatively safe training aircraft with good low speed flying characteristics should be utilized for carrier pilot training. The Curtiss SNC was considered unsatisfactory for the purpose and the SNJ-3 was selected for its overall good flying characteristics, rugged construction and ease of adaptability to the tailhook installation. As soon as the requirements were drawn up, the hook design and stress analysis was done by NAF

In 1942 the Navy rapidly expanded its use of the SNJ for carrier training. Many SNJ-3s were quickly modified for carrier operations and training began immediately. Here SNJ-3C BuNo. 7002 heads for trouble over the catwalk of the *USS Charger* on November 2, 1942. *(USN/National Archives)*

The *USS Charger*, a CVE retained by the Navy to train British crews, became an east coast training carrier in 1942. Here SNJ-3C BuNo. 7003 balances itself delicately on one prop blade which is stuck in the wooden deck following a barrier crash by Ens W. R. Davidson, USNR, on November 20, 1942. *(USN/National Archives)*

Ens Chris Fox, USNR, pranged SNJ-3C BuNo. 01894 in the catwalk of the *Charger* on November 30, 1942. The tough J-Bird survived with only minor damage. *(USN/National Archives)*

(Naval Aircraft Factory) Philadelphia, Pennsylvania, utilizing a modified existing in-production hook (Grumman P/N 10149).

In mid-1942 an initial batch of 20 SNJ-3s was selected at random to receive the hook modification (ASC-33). Assembly and Repair (A&R) Pensacola was directed to accomplish the task and set about manufacturing the required units. Len W. Cobb, SNJ production supervisor at the facility during the war, well remembers the program. "We manufactured everything needed for this modification . . . hooks, hand made all the attaching hardware, manufactured all handles, cables . . . everything. The completed installation was as good as any retrofit installation done on any airplane anywhere."

The first batch of SNJ-3Cs, as they were designated after the hook installation, were rushed to CQ (carrier qualification) units in Miami and San Diego where ships like the *USS Charger* and *Bataan* were used for CARQUAL (carrier qualification) training. The initial success of the SNJ-3C, and attrition, prompted an order for 35 additional -3Cs. As the training program expanded, the Navy realized a need for training ships devoted entirely to the qualification of carrier pilots. Thus, two Great Lakes steamers, the *C&B* and the *Greater Buffalo,* were converted to flat tops, becoming the *USS Sable* (IX-81) and *USS Wolverine* (IX-64). These two carriers, based at Navy Pier in Chicago, comprised the bulk of the Navy's training carrier capability. The planes were based at the Carrier Qualification Training Unit at nearby NAS Glenview.

Field Carrier Landing Practice (FCLP) was usually carried out at Libertyville and when the student was pronounced ready to CARQUAL, he waited at Glenview for the call to go aboard, or students went aboard by the busload early in the morning and took turns qualifying all day. The pace was generally hectic with each ship sometimes managing up to 180 landings an hour.

One gentleman well qualified to talk about these operations is Cdr Fred C. Durant, USNR

The *USS Nassau* swings into the wind with a deck load of West Coast CQTU SNJ-3Cs embarked in early 1943. All the Js are in fleet colors of blue grey on top and light grey on bottom as is the SOC parked near the starboard deck edge. The group of excited kibitzers in the foreground are standing in the after part of the island structure that became known as "Vulture's Roost." *(USN/National Archives)*

An SNJ-3C of the East Coast Carrier Qualification Training Unit roars down the deck of the *USS Charger* (ACV-30) on November 10, 1942. During the dark days of that year the Navy's desperate need for training decks could not be filled entirely by fleet CVEs, prompting conversion of two Great Lakes paddle steamers, the *Greater Buffalo* and the *C&B*, to the training carriers *Sable* and *Wolverine*. *(USN/National Archives)*

SNJ-4s of VN4D8, Barin Field, in April 1943 quite plainly show the wood fuselage monocoque—note the contrast of the polished metal fairing behind the rear seat gunner's hood and the dull aluminum paint on the rear part of the fuselage. Wood SNJ-4s were not modified into carrier versions unless the rear fuselage was first converted to metal. *(USN/National Archives)*

Two brand new SNJ-4s perform a section take-off on April 10, 1943, while assigned to VN4D8(VF), NAAS Barin Field, Foley, Alabama. *(USN/National Archives)*

The Chicago based *USS Wolverine* (IX-64) was commissioned in August 1942 for carrier pilot training in Lake Michigan. Here SNJ-3Cs and an SBD of the CQTU as NAS Glenview, Illinois, prepare for launch in January 1943. *(USN/National Archives)*

SNJ-3Cs and -4Cs being refueled on the *Wolverine* in southern Lake Michigan, spring 1943. A movie crew stands at the bow. *(USN/National Archives)*

The *Wolverine's* sister carrier, the *USS Sable* (IX-81), was commissioned on May 8, 1943 with the first carrier landing made by Ens Braun in an SNJ on May 29th. From that point on the two carriers operated almost continuously until war's end. Here an SNJ-4C and a batch of FM-2 Wildcats of CQTU Glenview await the passing of a storm aboard the *Sable* in June 1945—a storm fence can be seen in the foreground. *(USN/National Archives)*

(Ret) who served as flight deck officer on the *Sable* from July 1944 to December 1945. When interviewed by *NavAir News* in 1972 in his National Air and Space Museum office, Washington, D.C., Durant said "we usually commenced operations at 0800 every morning, seven days a week, depending on the wind. We ran downwind as far as possible if the wind was from the north, as it generally was, and turned around in time to catch the first group of aircraft from Glenview. On most days, a half hour before the carqualing aircraft arrived, the landing signal officer [LSO] would fly out. He would check with flight operations before taking his station on the platform. The LSO was part of Glenview's flight operations section and normally he had taken the students through the field landing practice.

"There were no hanger decks on either ship but, just ahead of the island on the starboard side, we had one or two outriggers which were T-shaped affairs. The LSO's airplane was simply backed onto one of them with the tail out over the water. The aircraft would come out to us in groups of five to seven and the LSO would bring them aboard for their landings. They each made at least five landings. As any old Naval Aviator knows, under the old system a cut was mandatory—you didn't take a waveoff on your own, you landed. Once the pilot got the cut, chopped the throttle, dropped the nose, flared out for a landing and caught a wire (there were nine hydraulically operated wires aboard *Sable*), the flight deck officer took over.

"As *Sable's* flight deck officer, I was the only person on deck at all times. My deck crews and tailhook men were in the catwalks. It was normal for the entire crew to duck each time a plane landed because the cable was pulled out and, in case it broke, they wanted to be out of its reach. I would run forward to get the attention of the pilot. Then, as I stood on the starboard side, I gave him the first signal—keep you feet off the brakes. When the cable had slackened sufficiently, I signaled him to hold brakes. The tailhook men would release the hook; the cable men would retract the cable; the barrier would be dropped. As soon as the deck was clear, I checked to be sure the propeller was in full low pitch position. As soon as the pilot nodded that he had checked pitch, I would visually check to see

An SNJ-4 begins its flare for landing. The white bars on each side of the star have been added in a darker shade of white and the aft letters are partially painted over. This often occurred when units repainted insignia to conform with directives in mid-1943. *(Bill Larkins via Jim Sullivan)*

The SNJ is credited with many firsts during its service life. This blue-grey/light grey -4, the first aircraft attached to NAS Patuxent River, Maryland, has just made the first landing at the new air station in May 1943. *(USN/National Archives)*

Mr. Len Cobb, Leadingman, AMG, A&R Pensacola, Florida, supervises J. R. Hardy, Apprentice, AMG, in turning up a freshly overhauled SNJ-4 (BuNo. 27759) on November 23, 1943. (Len Cobb photo)

that his flaps were in the full down position. We were then ready for turn-up. I held up my left hand, the signal to hold brakes, and also signaled to remind him to keep the stick full aft. Waving a small flag in my right hand, I would turn up the engine to full take-off speed. When I dropped the flag, the plane would take-off (there were no catapults). As soon as the aircraft was clear, the barrier was raised again and, ideally, at that point, the next pilot in the circle would be ready to land and receive his cut."

When SNJ-4s appeared on the scene, 45 of them were selected for the C conversion at Pensacola. Due to normal attrition and to maintain the overhaul pipeline, 20 more SNJ-4s were later done, followed by ten more designated for fleet units.

Not all of the SNJ-3s and -4s that received the tailhook installation during the war were formally redesignated as -3C or -4C. Many of these aircraft, perhaps as many as one fourth of the total, merely received a log book entry reflecting incorporation of ASC-33 (aircraft service change). The paper work stopped there. Likewise, many of the armed version of the plane never formally reflected a B designation either.

The tailhook was installed on those SNJ-4s with metal rather than wooden fuselage monocoques. In late 1944, 20 SNJ-5s were converted to -5Cs. After the war, a further 30 -5s were converted to replace those -3Cs and -4Cs scrapped. A further batch of -5Cs were sent to Argentina and, eventually, 30 more -5s would be converted to Cs in the late 1940s and early '50s. In addition, two SNJ-7s (BuNos. 90678 and 112314) were converted to -7Cs.

The only real problem ever encountered with the SNJ tailhook installation was an occasional failure of the tailhook uplock mechanism. Makeshift field fixes pending arrival of parts from

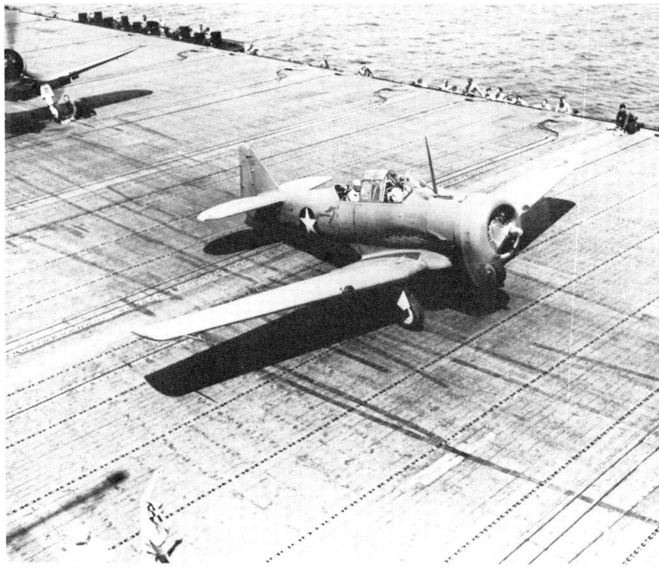

As the war progressed, many SNJs were sent to both coasts for use in carrier training workups and for general use of air groups and ships. This SNJ-4C, armed fore and aft (flexible gun is stowed), prepares to head for the beach from the *USS Bunker Hill*, July 1943. A VF-17 Corsair is next in line. *(USN/National Archives)*

An SNJ-4C in the barriers on the *Bunker Hill*, August 1943 The deck crew is trying to get the plane clear so others can land. *(USN/National Archives)*

Looking very much like the SBD Dauntless, and SNJ-4C clears the bow making the first take-off from the *USS Lexington* (CV-16) on April 22, 1943. *(USN/National Archives)*

The "Fly One" officer launches an SNJ for the beach with a passenger and mail from the *USS Nassau* (ACV-16) on March 8, 1943. The tail hook uplock latch is apparently broken on this J and the hook is tied up with a temporary cord. *(USN/National Archives)*

An SNJ-4 makes another first on a fleet carrier—this J has not received a C designation as of yet. *(USN/National Archives)*

By the spring of 1944 it was hard to find a place where the Navy did not use SNJs. This -4C departs the *USS Kasaan Bay* in May 1944. *(USN/National Archives)*

Pensacola involved bypassing the cockpit hook handle with a GI issue rope strung up the fuselage on the outside of the airplane. When the deck crew would reset the hook in the up catch, the rope was pulled taut and the pilot wrapped the rope around the armrest in the cockpit to hold it there. To lower the hook, one merely had to let the rope go slack to free the uplock catch. This problem was resolved and a standardized hook up/down handle was eventually designed and mounted at shoulder level on the upper right rear side of the pilot's cockpit.

A navy pilots' first carrier landing has always been a most memorable occasion in his flying career, leaving impressions that last a lifetime. This experience was repeated many thousands of times during the service life of the SNJ. Cdr Paul A. Ludwig, USN (Ret) recalled one such event when he qualified on the USS Monterey in the 1950s, something never to be forgotten. "I was a 'walk-aboard' when the carrier departed land and was in the Ready Room at sea when someone told me I was to man a plane on the hanger deck. For some reason today I can recall that the order came as a surprise since the atmosphere in the Ready Room was anything but organized. I remember getting in and fastening the straps in the gloom of the hanger deck. The Before Start check list was nowhere to be found. Panic set in a I searched under the seat after removing my straps because suddenly the gloom gave way to open ocean. The aircraft had been spotted on the aft elevator and while I was rummaging around the cockpit floor me and my plane were being lifted onto the flight deck. You can imagine that after months of indoctrination of check lists and organization and preparedness that the loss of the check list was a major theft of my security blanket.

"I vaguely recall a voice coming from my headset shouting at me to start my engine. It was the nearness of the voice that startled me while I came to the realization that my beloved check list was not going to get the engine started. Turning the battery on brought the voice. Turning the battery on meant I had accepted starting the engine alone without the printed word and now, suddenly, someone was shouting at me to get off his damn ship.

"Perched as we were, me and my SNJ, 45 feet above the entire ocean on a postage stamp of solid metal charging across the water and giving me a stiff breeze woke me up further from the previous world of check list security. I was going to fly off a carrier. It was a hell of a sobering thing. All those movies we Cadets watched in a dark, quiet and dusty training building for an after-lunch class entitled 'Naval Indoctrination' were merely movies now. All the stillness of the classroom and the filmed heroics of those World War II aces in their F6Fs gave way to reality.

"It was a bright summer day on the Gulf of Mexico and the movement of the USS Monterey produced a lively breeze. In every direction was real water and vivid colors. Everything had always worked before with my SNJs and I had taken off and landed dozens of times in FCLPs at Barin and outlying fields in just the same kind of salty and breezy Florida air. I recall putting things out of my mind. There was only one thing to do. My life had no other purpose or meaning at that moment except to make six traps and six launches. The only things which were new to me were the ship, the ocean, the wires on the fantail and the reality of doing the one thing which separates Naval Aviators from all others.

"The reliable Pratt & Whitney started the first time and I let the mental habits take over as my hands obeyed the months of preparations for take-offs. Everything went right. I was taxied forward, given the run-up signal and the go signal.

"The suprising thing about the carrier take-off is the lack of ground speed achieved when the thing starts flying. There was so much wind over the deck that we were in the air before the end of the deck came up. I had to force myself to believe we would stay in the air when it seemed that the trip up the deck was so slow. Suddenly, we were all alone over the ocean. I've never really liked water or being over it, much less having it be so deep with me strapped to 5,200 pounds of metal, supported only by an engine, a prop and some wings.

The SNJ could be a handful of airplane to control on the ground—these poor guys are being indoctrinated in the art of the ground loop by this VN5D8, Bronson Field SNJ-5 in late 1944. The tailwheel is unlocked and the plane is arcing to the right—the left wing is beginning to buckle. *(Jim Sullivan)*

If a loss of control upon landing didn't end up in a ground loop, it usually resulted in running off the runway and a noseover. This salvage crew at Corpus Christi, Texas, in August 1945 is busy trying to recover a J without further damage. *(USN/National Archives)*

A flight of SNJ-4s and an SNJ-5 attached to Carrier Aircraft Service Unit (CASU) 23. After the war, CASUs became FASRONs (Fleet Aircraft Service Squadrons). *(Roger Besecker*

"I got the gear and flaps up, timed my upwind turn and shot downwind, getting gear, flaps and hook down just in time to begin the final turn and to pick up Paddles. When I say we got on the deck I realize I leave out a lot of brief and mundane history. It is not dodging the truth to say that I had my mind swept clean of observations of the world around me and filled with extreme concentration. Things happened fast and in sequence. I had to get on the deck properly, safely and in a manner to bring credit upon a host of instructors, not to mention my peers and myself, or to say that a flub here would bring washout just at the moment of doing that one thing which makes Naval Aviators.

"Paddles gave me his signals and I got a wire. The first landing seemed too easy. Rather than shout for joy I took a firmer grip on the stick. There had to be a flaw. Things had gone as planned. One second of lack of concentration and I'd be in the water—or worse, I'd be put ashore and dropped from the program. I couldn't face making myself be washed out by error or lack of concentration. There would be time for fun in the fleet. I had to get those Wings.

"I got the second take-off, got a wire, third, fourth, fifth, and finally, last. It all went so fast and so well I felt superior. But all I had done was do what had been practiced and taught. It had been done by thousands before me. Still, there is that feeling which comes from accomplishing what one set out to do—to be with the people he wants to be with who had gone before him. I had always wanted to be a pilot on a carrier. Of course things still lay ahead such as a seven month tour at sea where one deals with isolation and lack of emergency landing fields. But combat and flying for hours over water aren't thoughts which come to someone in his first carrier approach. Not screwing up is what I thought about."

Tailhooked SNJs proved a boon to Navy fleet units—air groups, fleet carriers and seagoing staffs soon found many uses for the plane other than as a trainer. Several were assigned to ships and CASUs (Carrier Aircraft Service Units) for proficiency use and as all around hack airplanes. Often during sea trials of new carriers, the honor of the first carrier landing was usually reserved for the ship's CO, XO, Ops or Air Boss flying an SNJ onto such great ships as the *Yorktown* and *Bunker Hill*. These SNJs were usually painted in fleet colors and were either assigned to the ship for a time or to the shore activity supporting the ship. Such chores as mail runs and emergency leave transportation for ship's company personnel usually fell to the hook equipped J-Birds, flying between the beach and carriers training close to the shores of the U.S. or Hawaii.

The honor of first landings aboard new naval air stations, both stateside and overseas, sometimes fell to the J as well. Usually an SNJ was the first aircraft assigned to the new air station and was based nearby until the field was completed. As the concrete dried, it was not unusual for the new station XO or Ops officer to hassle each other for the chance to make the first tire marks on the new runway.

The Navy also made much use of the SNJ in rear areas overseas, sent over in fleet colors to be used as hack aircraft by those personnel attached to the base or by tenant commands. Bases in the Caribbean, the Canal Zone, South America, the Fijis, Alaska, Australia and verious islands in the South and Southwest Pacific usually possessed an SNJ or two by late 1944.

The Marines undoubtedly utilized the SNJ to the ultimate of its versatility. Historically, the Marines flew every model of the J-Bird and, in general, flew them longer than anyone else. They found an incredible variety of uses for the aircraft during World War II which varied from the standard pilot proficiency airplanes to close support training with ground troops, artillery spotters, message drops and pickups during troop training, photo training, and airborne wireless training; you name it, they either did it with an SNJ or were thinking about it when the war ended.

The outstanding overseas use of the SNJ fell to the First Marine Air Wing based in Noumea, New Caledonia, from October 1942. At least six SNJ-4s, among them BuNos. 05668, 09863, 09865, 09866 and 09873, flew from a small airstrip coded Magenta. Maj A. J. Bibee, USMC (Ret), at the time a member of the Advanced Surface Echelon of VMD-154, recalls, "The aircraft were used for the hauling of passengers, mail, aerial inspections of ground installations and camouflaged areas around Noumea Harbor and aerial photography missions. All airfields on the island of New Caledonia were photographed vertically from 10,000 feet and obliquely from cardinal points at 2,000 feet using a 12-inch K-17 camera. Several airfields in the northern part of the island were in the hands of the Vichy French but no ground fire was received."

In mid-December the SNJs were moved to Espirito Santo in the New Hebrides where Headquarters, Marine Air Group 11, operated them from the Turtle Bay Fighter Strip. In addition, one SNJ-4, BuNo. 26507, was received by VMD-154 in March 1943 and was operated by them for a considerable period. VMD-154 flew from Bomber One at this time, equipped with PB4Y-1P aircraft and the single SNJ. VMD-154 also operated Liberators from Henderson Field and Koli Point on Guadalcanal. "The SNJ was used primarily for the continued training of aerial photographers attached to VMD-154," related Bibee, who flew this aircraft a great deal during the period as well as completing many photc missions in the PB4Y.

The Marines operated every model of the SNJ, from the early versions prior to World War II to the late 1950s. SNJ-2 BuNo. 2034 of Base Air Detachment, Marine Base Quantico, Virginia, awaits refueling in early 1941. *(USN/National Archives)*

A Marine SNJ-3 of the 1st Marine Aircraft Wing in fleet colors of blue grey and light grey with red and white tail stripes. *(USMC)*

In the spring of 1943, exercises were conducted with a Marine Raider Battalion on Espirito Santo, where photos were taken for possible Battalion landing sites. On several occasions the SNJ was used to photograph exercise progress from the APD to the beach and on inland. At times the trusty SNJ even "played" enemy air. In addition to all this, remembered Bibee, the J-Bird was used by 154 pilots to keep current in single engine aircraft and for instrument training. It seldom needed maintenance.

SNJ-3 BuNo. 7008 involved in an in-flight message pickup exercise, April, 1942. Marine pilots and aircraft were attached to VMD-2, NAS North Island, San Diego, California. *(Al Bibee)*

Marines of VMD-2, North Island, mount the rear gun in SNJ-4 BuNo. 08974 on July 20, 1942. VMD-2 was originally formed as a Marine photo squadron (MPS-2) at North Island, then split from VMO-251 in April 1942. Later redesignated VMD-2, which later became VMD-154 in October 1942, the squadron was assigned to the 1st Marine Air Wing for overseas assignment. *(Al Bibee)*

An SNJ-4 operated by HQ MAG-11 takes an aerial camera abroad prior to a photo training mission, Turtle Bay, Espiritu Santo, New Hebrides Islands, in October 1943. *(USN/National Archives)*

A Marine SNJ-4 undergoing maintenance at Nandi Bay, Fiji Islands, in July 1943. The absence of rivet detail on the aft fuselage area indicates this is one of the SNJ-4s produced with a wood aft fuselage. *(USN/National Archives)*

An HQ MAG-11 SNJ-4 trundles down the runway behind an SBD passing a TBF and other SNJs parked under the palm trees at Turtle Bay, Espiritu Santo in 1943. *(USN/National Archives)*

MSgt A. J. Bibee, USMC NAP, disembarks from SNJ-4 BuNo. 26507, Bomber One Strip, Espiritu Santo on May 17, 1943. This aircraft belonged to VMD-154 which operated six Marine PB4Y-1Ps as well from the strip. *(Al Bibee)*

Although the official Marine Corps caption states that this picture was taken on Guadal Canal on 21 April, 1943, it is doubtful that SNJs were based at Cactus during this stage of the war. The primative working conditions do suggest a rear echelon base in the southwest Pacific.

An HQ MAG-11 SNJ-4 over Espiritu Santo in the summer of 1943, painted in the blue grey/light grey scheme of the period. *(USN/National Archives)*

As can be seen from the cowl gun in 51847, the installation was well designed and easy to maintain. Note the gun sight glass behind the windshield. *(USN)*

The rear seat flexible .30 caliber gun in the firing position on 51847. The system worked well after minor changes were made in the ammunition feed box mounting. *(USN)*

The wing gun installation on the AT-6/SNJ series was standard for the day. The gun functioned well but was seldom used by USN training units. *(USN)*

In September 1943 a Navy detachment visited Button, New Hebrides, to demonstrate to single engine pilots evasion of attacking enemy aircraft when flying alone. Two Navy SNJ-4s (BuNos. 27266 and 27558), flown by Lts Games and Lamar, were used to show the simple technique—cage the directional gyro on a cardinal point and head for the nearest cloud. Upon entering the cloud, the gyro was uncaged and evasive turns made within the cloud to lose the enemy. One of these aircraft, besides having a wood rear fuselage, was equipped with an experimental magnesium stabilizer.

As Naval Aviation moved out of the World War II era and into the immediate post-war wind-down, SNJs, along with thousands of other Navy training planes and service types, suffered an inglorious end in the smelter's furnace. The Navy kept most of the newer model Js but all remaining -2s and -3s, and even some -4s and -5s, were ferried to disposal depots and were either sold as surplus or were broken up for scrap.

To the average Navy flight instructor, this period held great confusion. Bases were closing at a great rate, training was being shifted rapidly from one base to another with very little warning and one wondered just where the whole program would finally sift out. No one in the training command knew how small the new peacetime training effort would become. The only painfully obvious display as each outlying base closed consisted of planes consolidated on the remaining fields or being flown out to disposal depots in great numbers.

"During this period," recalled Capt H. W. "Hec" Davis, USN (Ret), "the N2S units at Cabiness and Rodd had SNJs for instructor proficiency, which mostly were used for weekend cross countries. In addition to instructing, I was involved in ferrying many of the training command airplanes to bases where they were turned over to the War Assets Administration for disposal. The planes consisted mostly of SNVs, SNJs, NH-1s, N2Ss and SNBs. I ferried SNJs to Dos Palos (near Fresno, California), South Weymouth, Massachusetts, and Ellyson Field, Pensacola.

"In July 1946 I ferried an SNJ to Ellyson. The plane was recently out of overhaul. After I landed, I turned in the log books and headed for my ride back. I encountered a man who had been sitting on a bench just outside the hangar. He asked what shape the plane was in, how many hours on it and how much gas was in it. I told him the bird had just come out of overhaul at Corpus, had only ferry time on it and still was half full of fuel. The man walked over to the office, handed over $400.00, picked up the books and papers, climbed into the plane, which still had a warm engine and took off. Not bad for practically a zero time SNJ, even in 1946. I also saw a low time SNJ sold in Dos Palos for $1,100.00."

Bargains like these abounded after the war and many hundreds of SNJs found new homes in the hands of civilian owners. The Navy kept enough of the later model SNJs to meet training needs for the foreseeable future. New training concepts would soon evolve which were to change the flavor of Naval Aviation training for years to come, in that all primary and basic flight training would be done in one type aircraft—the SNJ.

In 1946, a move to modernize and upgrade Naval flight training was undertaken and, for a time, the Navy actually had three separate syllabi to test their new concepts. First was the proven one used at the end of the war—solo,

The wing bomb installation on 51847 developed minor problems with the larger size bombs during release. The SNJ was not suitable for dive bombing due to lack of a dive brake to keep speeds below red line. *(USN)*

As World War II drew to an end, many bases closed and the training syllabi were under constant revision. At war's end, these SNJ-5s of VN3D8A, South Whiting Field, Milton, Florida, maintain the training pipeline at a reduced pace. The syllabus at Squadron 3 was basic instruments, radio and formation. *(via Chet Bartusiak)*

After World War II, many SNJs were sold surplus—this one is a −4 which served with VN15D8 at Kingsville and has just been bought in outstanding condition, evidence of a recent overhaul. *(Eleutherian Mills Historical Library)*

A highly polished SNJ-6 attached to an admiral's staff at NAS Alameda, California, provides some proficiency for staff pilots in March 1947. Note the gloss blue anti-glare panel and spinner with gold pinstripe trim. *(Bill Larkins)*

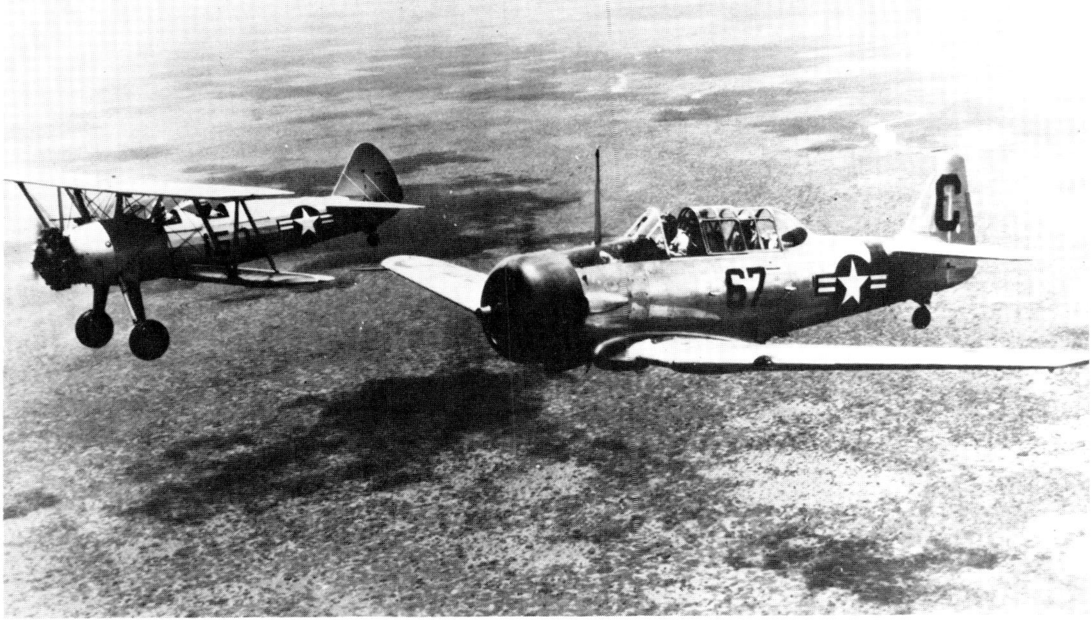

In 1947 the SNJ relieved the N2S of its duties as a primary trainer—this is the farewell flight but the Stearman was used through early 1948 for inverted spin training. *(NASM)*

acrobatics and formation flying in the N2S Stearman, then on to basic in the SNJ. The second was called "Project X-ray"—solo only in the N2S (about 10 hours) then go right into the SNJ. Third was "Project Yoke"—start right out in the J-Bird.

"All three methods worked fine," according to Hec Davis. "Naturally there was a loud cry that it would be too complex and difficult for students to start out in anything as big and hot as the SNJ. BALONEY!" History was to prove otherwise. In its new role as a primary trainer the SNJ helped prove that the new training concepts were right. The plane possessed no dangerous habits or unsatisfactory flying characteristics which would make it other than an excellent primary trainer. Many thousands of Navy student pilots received their first taste of Naval Aviation and their first solo in the venerable J-Bird.

Ted Thompson was ordered to Navy Flight Training at Pensacola in June 1951, fresh from the Naval Academy as an Ensign, and started at Whiting "right off in the SNJ and I soloed after 30 hours in a month. It was far easier to master take-offs, landings and flight than taxiing the J with a swiveling tail wheel. We likened it to learning to ride a tricycle backwards, while steering with your feet."

Those turbulent post-war days in Corpus Christi produced a humorous incident involving Tom Schaaff (later Cdr, USN) who was one of the first aviation midshipmen designated under the V-5 post-war program. On a particularly inky black Texas night, Tom was shooting night touch-and-go landings out of Cuddihy near Corpus. There were many planes in the air and the pattern was strung out for miles upwind. Just after turning downwind, Tom saw, to his horror, another SNJ coming head-on. Instinctively, Tom whipped the bird over and down, narrowly missing the other plane. As he righted his J-Bird on instruments (there was no horizon), he felt the plane fly into the ground.

The J proceeded to self-destruct as it slid along in the dark. When all the grinding, crunching, tearing and banging stopped, he realized he wasn't seriously hurt and stepped out of what was left of the aircraft. He felt around in the dark and noticed everything was gone from the firewall forward—nothing remained aft of the rear seat and both wings were gone. The center section with the mid-fuselage was sitting upright, all by itself, in a cotton field. Tom waited by the plane for awhile thinking that he would soon be missed and rescued. No such luck—flying was secured shortly thereafter and all was quiet. He just couldn't believe that no one would miss him so in the wee hours of the morning, he finally decided that he had better hike to a telephone and let the base know of his predicament and that he was OK.

Tom dutifully retrieved his tattered parachute from the seat and started hiking across the Texas boon docks in the dead of night. Eventually, he found a lone farm house where he promptly marched up to the front door and gave a resounding rap. The shock of the farmer and his wife, seeing this disheveled creature, all bruised and battered in a filthy, ripped to shreds flight suit at that hour of the morning was almost indescribable. When those folks regathered their composure it was found, fortune of fortunes, there was no telephone.

The kind folks decided to drive Tom back to base, arriving at Cuddihy main gate around 0400 in the morning. Tom's troubles, it seemed, had really just begun. The Marines at the gate immediately put poor Tom on report for: 1) being AWOL, 2) being out of uniform on liberty, 3) conduct unbecoming an officer by attempting to lie his way onto base with a big cock and bull story about a plane crash. A quick check with the squadron duty officer revealed that indeed no crash had occurred and all planes were accounted for. The plane was never missed. Further attempts by Tom to explain the situation only got him into deeper trouble. Finally, the decision was made to throw this wretched, miserable looking Midshipman, who had obviously been on liberty, had been drinking and had been in a fight, in the Brig.

It took some doing for Tom to get the guards to awaken his base OD (officer of the day) and come down to the Brig for a look. Tom pleaded with the officer to alert the squadron and for someone to physically go out on the flight line and count the SNJs. This was done and sure enough, one was missing. "Thank God," thought Tom. "They finally believe me and I'll have a doctor look me over and I can get to bed." But it was not to be. By now, the whole base was awake and all sorts of officer type folks, including the base commander, were wanting to know how a squadron could lose an SNJ, not to mention its pilot, and no one would know it. The most obvious question came next. Where was this alleged mangled SNJ? Not even Tom could answer that one. At first light, naturally (when else would the Navy do anything, several old Navy heads have since remarked), a large safari departed to search out the missing airplane with Tom Schaaff up front in true Stanley and Livingston fashion. The J-Bird was finally found . . . and Tom free to have his wounds cared for. Such a classic snafu elsewhere? Only in the military.

By the late 1940s the SNJ had established itself as one of the grand old aircraft of Naval Aviation. During this period, preflight school was 16 weeks with two weeks of officer candidate training on top of that, so the Aviation Midshipmen and Aviation Cadets who reported to Pensacola had a long way to go before actually climbing into a cockpit.

To those of us in Aviation Midshipman Preflight Class 14-48-4* standing at attention in the hot Florida sun on the parade grounds at Pensacola in June 1948, the sight of a sleek, silver SNJ passing low overhead to land at Chevalier Field was indeed a welcome reward. Actually, to most of us the first introduction to the SNJ came in the form of the Dilbert Dunker in the swimming pool. Midshipmen were mercilessly strapped into the cockpit section of an SNJ, to ride the beast down an incline into the water, where it promptly turned over and sank. The trick was to get yourself out and to the surface in quick time. This piece of survival training has no doubt saved the lives of more Navy pilots than any other single item besides the parachute.

The midshipmen were sent to Whiting Field, Milton, Florida, upon completion of Pre-flight training and here they met the SNJ face to face. BTU-1A flew from North Whiting and BTU-1B from South Whiting. After one taxi hop, called the LO, "A Stage" began in earnest. The author was assigned to North Whiting and how well I remember my great, hard-working instructor, Lt(jg) Davis. I progressed well through the syllabus and finally soloed the J-Bird at site "8 Able," a square grass field near Milton. "A Stage" at Whiting was approximately 27 hours long and solo came after the A-19 check or approximately 20 hours. I then progressed to "B Stage" at Whiting where we had a chance to build up our confidence and our basic skills for the next 23 hours.

This part of our training was very exciting. We had become proficient in simulated low and high altitude procedures, crosswind landings, lazy eights and high speed stalls. I do recall that crosswind landing practice proved exciting at times, both to the instructors and students alike. On more than one occasion I noticed a J-Bird sitting on an outlying field with a bent gear, prop and wing tip, the victim of an improper crosswind technique.

Occasionally we would see an accident that would really sober us up. I was following another SNJ at Milton T when I noticed that the student leveled out high, stalled, dug in a wing tip and cartwheeled for about 200 feet. When the plane stopped it was in pieces. The cockpits were sitting on the center section, the aft fuselage was gone, the other wing half gone, and the

*Coauthor Ohlrich was in this class.

Aviation Midshipmen man their SNJ-5Cs for carrier qualifications (CQ) aboard the *USS Wright* in December 1948. The −3Cs and −4Cs had been retired by this time. *(USN/National Archives)*

An SNJ-5C receives a cut signal at the ramp aboard a training carrier near Pensacola, 1948. Carrier training of student pilots in the SNJ continued to receive heavy emphasis until the final phaseout of the J in the late '50s. *(USN/National Archives)*

An SNJ with stubbed toes at Corry, April 18, 1950. The switch from steerable to locking/full swivel tail wheels after the war helped the ground loop problem to some extent but the ole J-Bird still demanded full attention on landing. *(R. M. Tvede, Jr.)*

engine was torn off at the firewall. The main injuries to the student and instructor were sore ears, from banging their heads on each side of the canopy glass. I began to realize the ole J-Bird was one tough machine, and was not only well designed, but well built.

The skipper of BTU-1A was LCdr "Red Horse" Meyers who would later become my commanding officer in VF-171. In Naval Aviation one finds familiar faces throughout one's career, building a comaradery that lasts a lifetime and that transcends much of the Mickey Mouse involved in being career military.

After 23 hours of "B Stage," I reported to BTU-2 at Corry Field where some real fun began. "C Stage" consisted of 25 hours of acrobatics and night flying—I delighted in learning how to put the bird through its paces. We ran the whole gamut of acrobatic maneuvers except one. Our SNJs were placarded against snap rolls. Then on to "D Stage" where, for the next 30 hours or so, my classmates and I wrestled with the SNJ from the rear seat under the hood to learn instrument flying. I had more trouble here than I did in any other phase of flight training. I'm sure that had it not been for my instructor, Lt Diamond, who was a prince of a fellow and above all a very tolerant, patient person, I would never have survived the instrument stage.

Two of my original classmates, Midshipmen Marv Quaid and C. J. "Obie" O'Brien, were struggling through instruments at Corry along with me and I remember us trying to console each other at the end of the day's flying activities. One of our major headaches was the infamous "Charlie Pattern." Who could ever forget it after once being forced to master instrument coordination and timing through it.

The Pattern itself, as I recall, had two minute legs, either climbing or descending and various 270° and 450° turns, either climbing or descending. To the novice pilot sweating under the hood in the Florida sun it was a real nightmare. Most of us eventually "lucked out" and passed our D-16 check ride with the usual "Santa Claus" check pilot who would hum "Santa Claus is Coming to Town" on the interphone as we returned to Corry.

We always wondered how the instructors could see out of the back seat of the thing. At the time, it made me feel like the instructors possessed some sort of supernatural instinct to survive all the hairy goings-on in the front cockpit.

BTU-3 at Saufley Field was, perhaps, the one place where the Midshipman had the best time. Most of our flights were solo and we began to have confidence in our ability to do something with the airplane. "E" and "F Stage" consisted of 60 hours of formation, cross country, both day and night, aerial tactics, including our first taste of combat maneuvering and aerial gunnery. The pace quickened and we flew two or three times a day.

My first cross country, to Selma, Alabama, was an absolute horror story . . . I was lost most of the way. I finally blundered across the Air Force base at Selma, then lined up on the wrong runway for the break with three other guys who didn't know where they were either. As we taxied in, I heard my instructor, who was in a chase plane, apologize to the tower for those four idiots who were all going to kill themselves. It sure made us feel like fools and as for myself, I realized I had a lot to learn about flying.

We practiced formation flying for what seemed like endless hours, until we became very good at it. One afternoon, we heard the crash siren sound and I saw a disabled SNJ heading straight in for landing. He landed normally, then the engine stopped on the runway. I watched as the bird was towed in and when we ventured a close look at it, I couldn't believe my eyes. Most of the center section, including one or both fuel tanks and part of the underside of the right wing had been sliced open as if by a giant can opener. I later learned that another J had over run this one on a rendezvous and crossed too closely underneath. The propeller cut through the center section like butter and the plane went straight into the ground, the first fatality in our happy group. This type of flying demanded much respect and care—an accident such as this made us *very* careful indeed.

My first tactics hop was a great laugh for my instructor. Each student was supposed to line up, nose to nose, but with a 1,000 foot altitude advantage to the student. The object was for the student to maneuver onto the tail of the instructor. I just couldn't believe that after a few high G turns and reversements I had the instructor glued squarely on my tail. There seemed to be nothing I could do to dislodge him, even with an accidental high speed, nose high stall where the bird whipped over the top and scared the liver out of me. I recovered and looked back. There he was, sitting back there grinning at me. I suppose every fighter pilot goes through this humiliation but back on the ground I vowed to learn the basics in aerial combat and learned them well, which I did. On a few succeeding flights I did manage to nail my instructor, but very seldom.

"F Stage" gunnery provided many new thrills. How could one ever forget that .30 caliber Browning machine gun going off right there in the cockpit. The gun was mounted in the upper

NAAS Corry Field looking across the east field met from the tower. By this time the SNJs were painted all-silver. BTU-2 acrobatic trainers are in the background while instrument trainers with high visibility green bands are in the foreground *(USN/National Archives)*

BTU-3, Saufley Field, gunnery trainers enroute to the firing range in the fall of 1948. *(USN/National Archives)*

An SNJ-5C flies up the port side of the *USS Wright* on November 3, 1948. In post-war years, USN CQ squadrons often removed the landing gear fairing doors because of the difficulty in keeping them in alignment with the constant pounding of shipboard operations. *(R. E. Bennett via Jim Sullivan)*

The *USS Wright* steams back into port to have this SNJ-5C removed from its port side, 1948. The J is hanging by its tail hook and a barrier cable. One can only imagine the reaction of the pilot as he hung, strapped in his seat, a few feet above the water, not to mention getting out. *(Walt Ohlrich)*

An SNJ-5C of CQTU-4 makes a nice landing on the *USS Wright* near Pensacola in the summer of 1948. Note the deck handlers standing in front of the cable at the deck edge. They are just beginning to move to the plane to disconnect the hook from the arresting cable once the J stops. *(Harry Gann)*

right side of the cockpit with the rear portion allowing access to the charging handle—after turning on the proper gun switches and hand charging, the gun was ready to fire.

Our gunnery flights consisted of four or five students and one instructor in the tow plane. We fired various colors of ammunition at a target sleeve taken aloft in a cannister under the right wing of the SNJ tow plane. He would stream the sleeve in the firing area and from right echelon, we would peel off, one at a time, and bang away at the sleeve when we were within range. This was great sport and, as I recall, we had to qualify with a ridiculously low number of hits—something like three percent. Even this was hard to do.

After the instructor dropped the sleeve at Saufley, we would gather around and count the various color holes in the sleeve, or lack of them. In my case, I seemed to be having a tough time getting the hang of it. I suppose I just wasn't pressing close enough to the sleeve before I fired, but that takes some getting used to. That gun would chatter away right in your face, or so it seemed, and the smell of burnt powder was quite strong.

I remember an incident on my last gunnery flight. It was supposed to be my final gunnery check flight before moving on to carrier qualification. My flight had fired out all our ammo and I felt that I had done reasonably well. As was customary, the last man off the target was supposed to circle back and join up on the sleeve to escort it home, the idea being that, hopefully, no other plane would fly between the two SNJs that had the tow cable stretched between them.

Loading ammunition in the cowl gun of an SNJ-5B at Saufley Field, 1955. Gunnery training in the J-Bird continued to the end of the aircraft's service life. Notice where the armorer has stuffed the gun cowling until he finishes. *(Paul Ludwig)*

A Marine SNJ-6 of VMT-2 (instrument training) over MCAS El Toro, California on July 5, 1951. In late 1950 new Navy paint specs called for the addition of the service name on the rear fuselage and moving the national insignia and squadron MODEX numbers farther forward on the fuselage. *(AAHS)*

On this occasion, our "smolderin' boulder" ace number four man decided to do a loop after his last run and join on the sleeve that way. He misjudged his distance, lost sight of the tow plane and sleeve coming down the backside of the loop and smartly cut the tow line as he plunged down ahead of the sleeve. I stared in disbelief as the ole sleeve shriveled up and dropped into the Gulf. Our hot rock midshipman was promptly dropped from the flight program for that little breach of discipline and the rest of us on that flight had to fly the hop over. I have always wondered if I had set a new gunnery record and in true Walter Mitty style, had my record breaking sleeve fall into the water. The refly went well, though, and I reported back to Corry the next day to CQTU-4 and Carrier Qualification training.

Carrier Qual was undoubtedly the most exciting thing that happened to me in the training command. By far it was the most challenging and rewarding experience of my flying career, as I'm sure it was for most fellows like myself who really wanted to be Navy pilots. All of our training thus far had led to this. The thought of landing the SNJ on the ship set my heart pounding with excitement.

Use of the SNJ at Saufley was drawing to a close when this photo was taken in 1954. BTU-3 moved to Barin Field where formation, gunnery and carrier qual continued. *(USN)*

"Bloddy Barin" takes it toll. A BTU-3 SNJ-5B, BuNo. 91001, lies crumpled in a field, July 1955. *(USN)*

After more ground school and two demo hops with an instructor, we started the endless hours of Field Carrier Landing Practice that characterizes a Navy pilot's transition to landing on an aircraft carrier. Most of us would ride the bus out to Bronson, Baghdad or Barin while the lucky ones would ferry six or eight SNJs from Corry and we would take turns in the FCLP pattern all day. In between flights, we would be debriefed by the LSO, wait our turn and go again with five or six planes in the pattern at once.

Flying low and slow took much practice. The most common errors were flying too high, above 60 feet, or too fast, above 65-68 kts. The trick was to set yourself up just past the 180° position, start a gentle left turn in and get your speed under control early in the pass. I found this to be hard work and I sweated profusely in the southern heat as I learned to slow fly the plane at 50 feet. I was pronounced ready for CARQUAL after 17 such flights. Told I would go aboard the *USS Cabot* in five days, I could hardly believe it.

During this time, I noted no SNJ accidents or mishaps throughout the entire FCLP evolution. The LSOs really knew their stuff. As luck would have it, I was chosen to fly out to the ship and our flight of six SNJs departed Corry early in the morning headed for the Gulf to rendezvous with the Cabot, a World War II CVL class ship which had departed Pensacola the evening before.

Our flight arrived and we orbited overhead as the ship made ready to take us aboard. As I looked down on that ship, my first look at a carrier from the air, my reaction was surprise. I'm going to land *this* airplane on *that* little thing? It looked like a 2x4 floating in the sea—gad, I began to have my doubts. All sorts of thoughts raced through my mind. A call from the ship jarred us all back to reality. Our flight had a Charlie Signal and as we started down, I saw the ship begin its swing into the wind. We dropped our tailhooks and proceeded up the starboard side on the Fox Corpen and each in turn broke downwind. I noticed how odd it felt to be low and slow over the water.

As I slowed down I dropped the wheels and then the flaps and ran over my landing check list, which in my SNJ-5C (BuNo. 51863) included the words Hook Down and Tailwheel Unlocked. The ship looked very pretty from this angle as I flew downwind . . . I checked my altitude by keeping the top of the stack on the horizon. As I passed the 180° position, I started my turn in and added a little power to keep my speed in the turn. I saw the pilot in front of me receive the cut signal from the LSO and he landed gracefully in the arresting gear.

The ship began to look bigger past the 90° position and as I approached the 45° position, I picked up the LSO. He signaled with a Roger, then went to a High. I eased the nose over and flew back down to the right altitude. I saw the plane in front taxiing forward . . . doubts set in about getting aboard. I assumed the deck would be fouled and I would get a waveoff for being too close. Turning into the groove, I received a fast signal, then a Roger from the LSO.

At this point the engine blocked out most of the view forward and I realized now why the Navy had drilled those turning approaches into us. You just can't see out of this bird on a low, slow, straight-in approach. Leveling my wings, I saw the Cut signal from the LSO—"well, here goes nothing," I thought as I closed the throttle and gently dropped the nose. As I neared the flight deck, I brought the stick full aft for flare—touchdown was three points and more gentle than I expected. I felt the hook catch a wire and the tail came up as the arresting gear brought the bird to a halt—hard against the shoulder straps but not violent.

As the plane slowed down, the tail dropped to the deck and I looked to the right to pick up Fly 3 as briefed. There he was, yellow shirt, giving me the signal to let the plane roll back, then to hold brakes. I saw the Hook Up signal and moved the hook handle to the up position in the cockpit to reset the hook uplock—then waited until the hook was repositioned by the deck crew.

Next signal—Taxi Forward. "Taxi forward?! Why can't they let me take-off from back here? That deck looks awfully *short*. Good grief, they are bringing me up abeam of the island!" I looked around the nose and saw the end of the flight deck about 300 feet away. "Aw, come on fellas. There must be some mistake."

I could hardly believe my eyes when Fly 1 signaled to check flaps down, then gave me the Wind-Up signal. I just gritted my teeth and shoved the throttle up to 26″ as briefed. Fly 1 dropped his flag and pointed down the deck. I released the brakes and went to full throttle. It took more right rudder than I expected as the bird accelerated. To my astonishment, the ole J-Bird started to fly before I reached the bow. As the flight deck passed behind and my trusty steed was pulling me away for another pass, I felt a tremendous surge of excitement and exhileration. The feeling was akin to my first solo. I had done it. I had landed aboard a Navy ship of the line and was well on my way to being a professional Navy pilot.

With heart pounding, I came around again and again until I had made the required six landings, after the last receiving the Switch Pilots signal. Climbing out, I ran for the deck edge and literally jumped for joy. Those Navy wings were coming closer and even though I would return in a few short months and land aboard the *USS Saipan* in the F6F-5 Hellcat, the feeling was not quite the same as the first trip aboard in the venerable SNJ.

I spent the rest of the morning observing flight operation from "Vulture's Roost" in the island structure. The entire show went so smooth I found it hard to believe. While having lunch in the Wardroom, however, one of the switch pilots joined us and said we were now going downwind while we disentangled an SNJ from the barriers, the only glitch in an otherwise outstanding day.

The early afternoon was devoted to advanced CQ in F4Us and F6Fs. Once again I was impressed at how smooth flight operations were on a carrier. In late afternoon, the SNJs came back and right away we had problems. One student lined up left, landed badly off center and tried to take a wave-off at the last minute. The plane went over the port side and hung there dangling just over the water held by the tailhook and arrester wire. That did it for the day. We headed back to Pensacola so we could get the J-Bird unstuck.

As the SNJs soldiered on in their primary role of training, the Navy continued to find increased uses for the trainer, the most important being proficiency flying. During the late 1940s and up to the mid '50s, almost every naval air station

102 NAVY
BA

NAVY
102
BA

Opposite page top to bottom
An SNJ-5C about to make an inflight engagement of the arresting gear cable on the *USS Monterey*, 1956. Engaging the cable in this manner usually resulted in an extremely hard landing with considerable airframe damage. *(USN via Bernie Karsh)*

Carrier landings have always posed a special brand of thrills. Here a CQTU-4 Barin based SNJ-5C is in extremis. The J is fully stalled, rolling to the right with full throttle unable to recover. *(Robert Lawson)*

The J-Bird continues to roll, striking its right wing on the deck as it heads for the water over the starboard side. The incident took place on the Monterey near Pensacola September 5, 1953. *(Robert Lawson)*

The "J" bird crashes nose down, inverted into the after stack. *(Robert Lawson)*

The plane comes to rest upright in the water minus engine. The pilot can be seen stepping out of the cockpit as the wreck begins to sink. *(Robert Lawson)*

in the continental U.S, and overseas was equipped with a few SNJs along with a hard working Beech SNBs. These planes were provided so the aviators attached to shore duty activities could maintain flight proficiency. The planes were attached to FASRONs (Fleet Aircraft Service Squadrons) on large Naval installations or to the air station itself. In areas where there were large concentrations of pilots, such as Washington, D.C. or the Naval Post Graduate School in Monterey, California, substantial numbers of these aircraft were provided. In 1956, the author was assigned to Monterey with proficiency aircraft that consisted of SNBs augmented by six SNJ-6s, two F8F-2 Bearcats and two AD-1 Skyraiders. The SNBs eventually replaced the SNJs due to their greater utility when the Navy increased emphasis on instrument flying for proficiency aviators.

The Navy usually had one or two SNJs assigned to each aircraft carrier in the fleet during the late '40s to mid '50s. Once again pilot proficiency was the name of the game with the ship's company aviators assigned to fly the J on a variety of missions including mail runs, photo missions, target tow and general utility. The J-Birds were taken on deployments overseas with the assigned Air Group and, when not flying, were stored in Hangar Bay #4 on CV class carriers. The Js were launched ahead of the Air Group and recovered last.

When the ship was due for a port call of any length, the SNJs were launched to the closest military field, where they would be based for the duration of the port stay. Ship's aviators, not currently carrier qualified in the plane, made use of them while ashore.

It was on one such occasion when our *USS Coral Sea* Js were based at Compodichino near Naples, Italy, in the winter of 1950, that the author was in some kind of deep trouble with U.S. and Italian authorities. I was assigned to the Air Group at the time, but did not have enough flight time for the month so I sweet talked the ship into letting me log some time in the SNJ-5Cs in Naples. Another squadron pilot went with me.

It seems, according to the local news media, a madman Naval Aviator (me) led a flight of two SNJs down into the Mt. Vesuvius volcano near Pompeii. It was feared those two noisy beasts clattering around in there would awaken the sleeping volcano as had happened in 1944. I'm sure it had been done before and at the time it was great sport—the ole tiger blood prevailed—no guts, no air medals. Of course we received a standard GI issue butt chewing and rest assured no more dumb stunts like that occurred the rest of the cruise.

Ship based SNJs served with Air Groups until the mid 1950s when replaced by AD-4Qs and TF-1s.

The training of Naval Aviation Reservists was one of the most important functions of the SNJ in service. It started back in the pre-World War II days when new SNJ-2s were assigned to Reserve units for instrument training. With time out during the war, the SNJs were pressed back into Reserve service immediately after the war. In fact, SNJs and SNBs were often the first machines taken on strength in newly formed Reserve squadrons until the arrival of service types.

In the late '40s SNJs attached to large Reserve air stations, such as Dallas, were flown to cities without existing Navy facilities such as Tulsa and local Navy Reservists would fly the planes all weekend. On several occasions I observed four to six SNJs on the line at the Air National Guard base in Tulsa. The Js were usually kept airborne most of the weekend being refueled, serviced and flown by local Reservists using ANG facilities. The J did not disappear from the Reserve training mission until the late '50s.

The Navy has long felt that the secret of an aircraft's long, successful service life is adequate maintenance, coupled with complete periodic overhaul. From the early days, Naval Aviation began to set up an overhaul program second to none. Assembly and Repair (A&R) was coined back in 1919 when planes were made of wood and fabric. Newly manufactured aircraft were shipped in crates from the factory to the Navy, where they were assembled and test flown by the A&R units. The A&Rs of the World War II era were a different breed of cat, however, dealing mostly with all metal aircraft and applying their manpower to airframe overhauls and in-service repairs. In addition, they performed engine and accessory components overhaul.

The A&R designation hung on until 1948 when the more appropriate Overhaul and Repair (O&R) was adopted. Most of the major A&Rs during the war, such as A&R Corpus Christi, were at one time or another involved in the overhaul or repair of in-service SNJs. Early in the war, A&R North Island, San Diego, California, published a unique photographic parts catalog of the SNJ-3, originally designed to facilitate aircraft overhaul. BuNo. 6863 was stripped down to its smallest part for this project, then parts were grouped together into various subassemblies which were photographed. The photos were then edited and indexed by group and part number in the catalog. The usefullness of this approach rapidly became evident in the maintenance of SNJs in squadron service, as more and more young and inexperienced maintenance person-

Clockwise from top
An SNJ-5C of CQTU-4 drones over Escambia Bay, near Pensacola, toward the end of the aircraft's service life. The words "DON'T STALL" are painted under the pilot's cockpit—not bad advice. *(USN/National Archives)*

Shortly after World War II ended, Naval Air Reserve units were reactivated around the country. This SNJ-5 sits on static display during an open house in 1946. *(Eleutherian Mills Historical Library)*

Reserve SNJs of the Oakland Naval Air Reserve fly over San Francisco Bay in 1948. Reserve Js were often taken along with the squadron during the two week active duty training deployments each year. *(NASM)*

In 1957 this −5 was still serving with the Willow Grove, Pennsylvania, Naval Air Reserve. Its replacement, a T-34, can be seen in the background. *(Roger Besecker)*

nel entered the Navy. The actual picture combined with the part number greatly aided maintenance training and reduced errors in ordering parts.

A&R North Island published this type of catalog on a great number of Naval aircraft during World War II—eventually, illustrated parts catalogs became the norm in the Navy but these all consisted of illustrated drawings of the various parts, not photographs.

The one facility in the Navy system most closely associated with the SNJ overhaul program was A&R Pensacola where NJ, SNJ involvement spanned 18 years. A typical trip through for an SNJ meant stripping the paint and dismantling the J down to the smallest components. All parts were examined for wear, damage or corrosion and refurbished, rebuilt, rebushed, corrosion treated and anything else necessary. In many cases, entirely new parts were manufactured at Pensacola to ensure a good product. Major subassemblies such as the fuselage monocoque, horizontal stabilizers, fins, wings and center sections were placed in alignment jigs to insure factory new tolerance throughout the aircraft's service life.

"We processed the SNJs through the assembly line process at an amazing rate during the war," remembered Len Cobb who was SNJ Production Supervisor at Pensacola for 15 years. "The assembly line, consisting of a number of work stations, moved every hour and 36 minutes. The crews worked by the big clock used to time the operation and as the clock moved past the hour and 36 minutes allotted, a whistle would blow, then each crew moved their dolly ahead one station. Every man knew his job so well that each assigned task was completed on time as the cycle came around again. The blowing of the whistle triggered an almost automatic reaction and we actually brought one plane in and shoved a completed one out the door every hour and 36 minutes, which amounted to about five planes a day.

"This vigorous pace was maintained throughout the war with our most active month in January 1945 when a total of 156 SNJs were inducted, overhauled, reassembled, test flown and delivered. A later peacetime milestone was reached when 318 SNJs were overhauled during the second quarter of 1950. The average time for an SNJ overhaul was 25 days induction to flight test," a figure that remained relatively constant during the '40s and '50s.

The initial service tour of the SNJ when received new by the Navy was 24 calendar months. Succeeding service tours between overhauls were 20 months in operating status but extensions to 22 or 24 months could be granted if the plane was in sound mechanical condition. The majority of the planes would rotate in on time, however, in order that the smooth flow of operating aircraft through the highly complex overhaul pipeline would not be disrupted. Aircraft in a pool status awaiting rarely exceeded 30 days.

When in the process of overhaul, the SNJs were also modernized and upgraded as necessary as the planes aged in service. It was the O&R responsibility to insure that all applicable Aircraft Service Changes, Service Bulletins, Tech Orders, Tech Notes and Aircraft Armament Bulletins were incorporated in the plane prior to delivery. Airframes that achieved four overhauls and five service tours were issued 60 ASCs, 61 Bulletins, 23 TOs, nine TNs, three AABs and 52 Local Specifications during their service life. The actual number of ASCs and TOs incorporated is less than the number assigned (which was small in itself) as many were cancelled, modified or never issued at all. The SNJ was built to last in the training environment, and last it did.

Some of the more interesting major modifications made by A&R Pensacola through Service Changes and Bulletins were ASC-33 (the arresting hook), 12 (replacement of the wooden horizontal stabilizers with metal) and 32 (replacement of the wooden fuselage monocoque with metal. ASC-32 took place in 1945 and early, '46 on those aircraft selected to be retained after the war. The wood monocoque structures had proved unsatisfactory and NAA manufactured and shipped hundreds of new units to Pensacola for installation on the -4s and -5s chosen.

"We had these large crates coming in on a monthly basis in late 1945," said Cobb. "The ordeal of opening them and storing the unopened ones became a problem when one is dealing with hundreds of units that large."

The task was completed by mid-1946 and all SNJs built with wooden control sticks, floor trays, seats, trim tabs, horizontal stabilizers and fuselage monocoques had them replaced. Those J-Birds sold surplus after the war with their wooden structures intact were not considered eligible for an airworthiness certificate by the CAA, which accounts for their quick disappearance from the American scene.

In the post-war era various sub designations of the SNJ were formally assigned by the Chief of Naval Operations. Although the C models had been so designated for some time, ACL (Aviation Circular Letter) 26-46, 14 February 1946, formally added the SNJ-5 and -6 to the basic C model designation and stated that the -3C, -4C, -5C and -6C would be equipped with arresting gear installations and radio equipment required for carrier operations. The SNJ-5B and -6B model designations were established on August 10, 1948, by ACL 73-48. It stated that these aircraft were basically the same as the SNJ-5 and -6 but would be equipped with a .30 caliber gun, gun sight, gun camera and ARC-1 radio equipment.

The most interesting SNJ modification done at Pensacola came with the -7, when the Navy decided to upgrade 50 Js to extend their service life beyond five service tours or five overhauls. The Bureau of Aeronautics, by letter dated 20 April 1951, directed that a pilot program be accomplished by O&R Pensacola to produce six prototype SNJ-7s using two SNJ-4s, two -5s and two -6s. Of the six prototypes, one was to be a gunnery (B) version and one a carrier (C) version. When all was said and done, the SNJ-7 was to be an updated airplane based upon the USAF remanufactured T-6G.

The final engineering details for the SNJ-7 configuration were, as later determined by NAS Pensacola, derived from a number of sources including recommendation by the Chief of Naval Air Training, BuAer specs and plans as well as NAA specifications for the T-6G. An order was placed for six T-6G change kits. O&R Pensacola finally inducted SNJ-4 BuNo. 27850 as the prototype -7B with a gun mounted in the right wing only; two SNJ-5s, BuNos. 90743 and 90678, which became -7Cs; and three SNJ-6s, BuNos. 112303, 112229 (which became a -7B) and 112314 which became a -7C. During the mod program, official correspondence listed these aircraft as SNJ-4-7BX, SNJ-5-7X, SNJ-5-7CX, SNJ-6-7X, SNJ-6-7BX and SNJ-6-7CX.

The program was slow getting started as very little emphasis was placed on the project by the Bureau of Aeronautics—by this time the Navy had its eye on new tricycle gear trainers, the T-28 and T-34, then on the horizon. They wanted to get rid of the SNJ as soon as possible. The SNJ-7 prototypes languished around the O&R modification hangar for many months until a definite effort was made to complete them. Although the aircraft were selected for conversion on February 21, 1952, and rework commenced between March and April, the first -7 was not completed and test flown until December 10, 1952, and the last was finally completed in April 1953.

Although the SNJ-7 was an excellent airplane and even much improved over the T-6G, the decision was made to stop the program. Thus, only the original six SNJ-7s were completed—two served with BTU-2 at Corry as instrument trainers, one with BTU-3 at Saufley and three with CQTU-4 at Barin. All the -7s went to storage at NAF Litchfield in November and December 1954, then stricken Category 4 on August 10, 1956.

This SNJ-6 served with the Blue Angels during their early days with the F6F Hellcat and F8F Bearcat. Painted yellow with a red Japanese insignia, the J-Bird was "shot down" during each show after a dogfight with the Grummans. The rear seat passenger would throw a parachuted dummy out and the J would stream smoke as it headed for the ground. *(Pete Bowers)*

The service career of the SNJ was long enough to have it involved in a number of interesting projects. SNJs and SBDs were used to test an experimental landing mat system in 1944. In early 1946 SNJ-3 BuNo. 05461 was involved in stability and roll rate tests at Pax River, equipped with a large accelerometer in both cockpits, a Schwein rate of roll indicator in the rear cockpit and an NACA Amers dial-gauge type stick-force indicator with a maximum indicating hand mounted on the front control stick. A total of nine hours of test time were flown satisfactorily and the J proved that accelerated tests of this nature would yield accurate results through the use of a few easy to install, inexpensive instruments. The project pilot on this experiment was a young lieutenant named N. E. Halaby, later to become FAA Administrator.

The Navy's flight demonstration team, the Blue Angels, used an SNJ in their show when they flew F6F-5 Hellcats and F8F-1 Bearcats as their show planes. From late June 1946 to September 1949, an SNJ-6, painted bright yellow with Japanese insignia, was a bogus Zero in a simulated dogfight with the F6Fs and F8Fs. The J, naturally, would lose the fight and be shot down, streaming smoke as a crewman in the back seat threw out a dummy, complete with parachute. Nicknamed "Beetle Bomb," The J was flown by Lt(jg) Gale Stouse until he left the team, then by any new pilot reporting to the team while he waited for an opening in the formation. It was used also for instrument training and as primary transportation for the team's narrator between shows.

Although the Navy did not experiment with use of skis on the SNJ as did the Army Air Force, the Navy did accomplish one of the most interesting experiments ever undertaken with the AT-6SNJ series aircraft. In 1952, as the peak of interest in successful hydro-ski experiments with the Convair XF2Y-1 Sea Dart, the Navy modified SNJ-5C BuNo. 51925 for sea trials. In conjunction with private firms working on hydro-ski programs such as the Edo Corporation and All American Aviation, the plane was tested with both single and double hydro-ski installations. The tests were conducted under the Patrol Branch, Naval Air Test Center, Pax River. The J's wings were coated with neoprene to provide flotation, if needed, and, as the program progressed, two large streamlined tanks were mounted under the wings inboard of the landing gear after it nearly dunked during tests under heavy loads. On the whole the program was sucessful, but the entire hydro-ski concept was abandoned and the trainer was converted back to a standard SNJ-5C.

By the mid-1950s, the heyday of the SNJ was on the wane. Many changes in Navy flight training had taken place since 1950 and with an increasing number of jet powered aircraft entering fleet service, the Navy was anxious to modernize its flight training with the introduction of a tricycle gear trainer. The old VND8 designations which would later become BTUs, then VTs, reflected a rapidly modernizing Navy.

As T-34s and T-28s were phased in, the SNJs started to disappear, initially at Whiting Field in July 1955. Eighteen months later T-34Bs had taken over the field. The thoughts and feelings of the instructors during the transition were summed up by Obie O'Brien, Cdr, USN (Ret), who served as an A, B and C Stage instructor with BTU-1N at Whiting. "The advent of the T-34 on the scene was greeted with great anticipation by the instructors. There was little or no remorse for the passing of the tried but very tired SNJ. The competition among the instructors to check out and start instructing in the T-34 was keen. The last instructional flight in the J was usually not a moment of regret and nostalgia but one of thanks and relief.

One of the more fascinating modifications made to the SNJ was the addition of hydro-skis. Here, the SNJ comes out of the water in the Chesapeake Bay during tests at NAS Pax River in 1952. Both single and dual skis were tried. *(Bill Larkins)*

The SNJ-5C used for the hydro-ski tests were BuNo. 51925. The wings were sealed with neoprene to keep the plane afloat in case it dunked. After a near accidental sinking, two large floatation tanks were added under the wing center section inboard of the landing gear. *(NASM)*

The end of the line. SNJ-5 BuNo. 43944 awaits its fate in the sun along with its sister ships at NAF Litchfield Park, Arizona, 1958. Many of the aircraft at Litchfield were sold to civilian owners for an average of $1,200 each in 1959. The rest went to the Military Assistance Program or were sold for scrap.. *(Roger Besecker)*

Like external sentinels guarding hallowed ground, these SNJs are quietly rusting away as of 1981 near the now queit Bronson Field, Florida. The SNJ did more to train two generations of Navy pilots than any other trainer built. *(Walt Ohlrich)*

"This feeling was fostered by a number of factors: 1) a new aircraft with everything working brings great comfort to the instructor, 2) in the T-34's rear seat, the instructor could see where his student was taking him, especially on takeoffs and landings, 3) although the T-34 could be groundlooped, it takes practice—not so with the SNJ, 4) cockpit environment was greatly enhanced in the T-34—the J's noise and lack of effective temperature control (especially in the rear seat) could produce one very tired and irritable instructor after the third or fourth flight of the day, 5) the tricycle landing gear was an enjoyable novelty to many instructors who had flown only taildraggers, 6) the customary bottle of firewater presented to the instructor by his student after his first solo was only 12 flights in coming with the T-34 versus 20 with the J-Bird. When I climbed out of the SNJ after my last instructional flight I did so with no regret. Had I only known how much I would miss her in the years to come!" By January 1957 the J was just a ghost at Whiting.

By the spring of 1958, the only SNJs remaining in the training command pipeline were those of VT-28 at Corry. On May 21, 1958, an historic echelon flight was made across Corry as the final training flight of the SNJ in the Navy, also marking the end of flight training on the field. After 36 years as a Navy training base, named after Medal of Honor winner and Naval Aviator #23, LCdr William M. Corry, Jr., the gates closed in July. The five pilots who made the flight were four students—Ens H. E. Heavener, W. L. Fluke, W. H. Gill, Jr., and Robert M. Clason led by their instructor and VT-28 Skipper, Lt Jim Mulligan, who later became famous as a long term POW in Vietnam. Jim had the honor of making the last landing at Corry, flying SNJ-5 BuNo. 90995 which was the last to leave Corry the next day for storage at Litchfield Park, Arizona. Interestingly enough, each of the last five planes had accumulated five overhauls—total flight time for the five Js amounted to 17,635 hours, the high time bird having 5,179 airframe hours.

According to Jim Mulligan, "the availability of the planes was absolutely outstanding to the end . . . never any maintenance problems at all." Certainly these are fitting words to a faithful airplane. Along with North American's SNJ went the taildragger training era in the U.S. Navy.

Chapter Three

Hot Rock Pilots and Terrible Texans

As the SNJ was to the Navy, so the AT-6 was to the Army Air Force in World War II and to the USAF after 1948 as the T-6. It was the first taste of what an honest-to-goodness operational type would be like—what a fighter would be like. And by all accounts, it didn't disappoint anyone. It would remain one of the more vivid periods in the life of Army and Air Force pilots.

With Army, Navy, British and other foreign contracts, North American had six different models of what began as the NA-16 under construction by early 1939. The AT-6 (NA-59) had come out of the BC-1A (see Chapter 1) and by the time the AT-6A (NA-77) was ordered under Army Air Corps Contract AC-15977 on June 28, 1940, North American had standardized the type as the AT-6A/SNJ-3/Harvard II, all rolling off the assembly lines at Inglewood together with different serial numbers. So similar were the Army and Navy products that both the AT-6A and the SNJ-3 were ordered under an Army contract and approved for both services by Army personnel.

When AT-6A/SNJ-3 production was transferred to the new NAA Dallas plant under the charge number NA-78, the aircraft would remain basically unchanged for the remainder of its service life. The only differences to speak of were related to the missions of each service—due to proximity to salt air, SNJs had their airframes, nuts, bolts and rivets zinc chromated and the interiors of the wings were coated with hot linseed oil.

When Harvard II production (see Chapter 4) started in Canada due to increasing demand for the type, Noorduyn Aviation Company, Ltd. began to build AT-6As as Harvard IIAs for lend-lease use by the Commonwealth nations. A part of the transaction involved 1,800 aircraft to be built with U.S. Army Air Force serial numbers for American use as AT-16s.

When the AT-6B (NA-84) was ordered on December 6, 1940, two basic changes were incorporated into the 400 Dallas-built aircraft. The Pratt & Whitney R-1340-AN-1 engine was installed, from this point on to be the standard engine for all examples of the type, and gunnery training provisions were completed. This was the last production version of the AT-6 that was ordered without being a part of SNJ line—until NAA stopped the line, the Navy and AAF versions would be linked under the same NA charge numbers (see Chapter 2 for a complete production run-down).

The only attempt by the Army Air Force to improve the high altitude performance of the type came in the form of the XAT-6E, an AT-6D modified to take a 575 hp Ranger V-770-9 inverted-V engine. Overall length was increased to 31 feet 1 inch and an honest 30 mph was gained in top speed but the Pratt & Whitney's reliability was greater and the project was terminated.

As the first AT-6s found their way into Army Air Corps units in 1940, it was evident a new generation of military aircraft was being introduced from the bottom up. The 36th Pursuit Squadron received some of the first production AT-6s for night and instrument training at Mitchel Field, Long Island—since the aircraft handled and performed like a fighter, the training was very realistic. Any fighter pilot who flew in those days with a bare minimum of instruments found night and instrument flying a real challenge—and it was one of the more neglected areas in AAC training.

In 1940 William H. Mann was an enlisted man in the 91st and 82nd School Squadrons at Maxwell Field, Alabama, when the first AT-6s arrived. The Air Corps Tactical School there was in the midst of the service-wide training build up, the first aircraft for basic training being BT-13s and 14s. The first aircraft for advanced training consisted of a mixture of AT-6s and BC-1As . . . "the BC-1A was used in the same formations with AT-6 since flight characteristics were the same except for the additional weight. We later always installed an R-1340-AN-1 for the [later] AT-6s in the BC-1A to give it the extra 50 hp. We were still using R-1340-47s, 49s, 51s and AN-1s in both aircraft when I left for a B-26 unit in 1942. Parts interchangeability was approximately 80% between the AT-6/AT-6A and the BC-1A.

"The aircraft had a great deal of utilization due in part to the simple design and the fact that the organization I was in had assigned an adequate share of the 'old timers' from the Air Corps Tactical School. I recall many of our aircraft logging 8 to 10 to 12 hours a day and in one incident having one with 18 hours out of 24. We had the usual problems such as shortage of spares, which accounted for 60% of our down time.

"The other problems I recall were: a) broken

ring cowl lugs on cylinders due to operation in low pitch with high power settings over too long a period and an over torque of ring cowl adjustors; b) some incidents of being unable to calibrate the magnetic compass due to the tubular structure of the fuselage becoming magnetized—this was solved by the depot after a demagnetizing facility was developed where the entire aircraft could pass through; c) cracked engine mounts—we checked the tubular mounts at engine change by pressurizing the interior with hot linseed oil or hydraulic fluid; d) cracked or bent struts, wing tips and flight surfaces due to ground loops.

"Many incidents come to mind—having 32 dead batteries after one aircraft was struck by lightning; they were parked wing tip to wing tip on the ramp. Apparently the static grounds didn't do too well on the concrete ramp. There were a number of accidents or loss of power due to misuse or not using the carburetor air. We had four fatalities in 30 days with the British cadets attempting to take-off with the carb air in hot position. I recall the whistling that identified an AT-6 with a prop that had a hole in both blades. We always had a few since we received serviceable props that had been balanced out after a gun got out of synchronization.

"I worked on the T-6 up through Korea, then ended my career in F-111s but I always remember the BC-1A and the T-6A through G as a most enjoyable aircraft to maintain."

Even though most U.S. leaders knew war was coming, December 7, 1941, had a devastating impact on every American, serving to galvanize the nation into a unified war effort. The last class of U.S. Army Air Force (changed from the Air Corps the previous June) cadets to graduate before Pearl Harbor was 41-I at Luke Field, Arizona. On December 6 the cadets flew a graduation formation fly past and then bolted for some well earned leave with their new silver wings. Jack Ilfrey, later an ace in P-38s and P-51s, recalled he was "at the Westward Ho House (Hotel) the Sunday morning of December 7th, 1941, when the loud knock of an MP rattled the door, with the announcement and ordering us back to Luke." These young 2nd lieutenants, including the author's father, Ervin C. Ethell, were thrown straight into preparing for war.

Until Pearl Harbor the AAF planned for 30,000 pilots a year, but by October 1942 that rose to 50,000, forcing planners to drop the college attendance requirement and several of the physical requirements. A potential Aviation Cadet still had to meet the following requirements: 18 to 27 years old; normal visual acuity, color perception and hearing; between 5′ and 6′4″ weighing 105 to 200 pounds (except for a fighter pilot who had to be 5′4″ to 5′10″ and 114 to 160 pounds). Many of the requirements could be waived, however, within limits.

Once accepted, the Cadet went to Pre-Flight Training which consisted of Basic Training and Pre-Flight School. Both areas were heavy with "military indoctrination" since the Cadet would receive his Primary Flight Training at a civilian contract school. Marksmanship, bivouac and survival, health, drilling, physical training and military procedure made up Basic in addition to medical, psychological and aptitude tests which determined aircrew assignments.

Those who made it to Pre-Flight were in for more military indoctrination, military customs and regulations, infantry drill, and physical training, but at last pilot trainees entered the world of study related to what they were dreaming of: math, physics, map reading, meteorology and aircraft and shipping recognition. Cadets also got a good dose of the upper class/lower class system with upper class cadets continually harassing their underlings, particularly through hazing which was officially stopped in May 1943 but unofficially encouraged by officers. According to William Wolf*, "The dining room was the favorite area for hazing. Lower classmen had to sit at attention at the dining table on the front two to three inches of their chairs sometimes with a cracker between their stomachs and table. In the 'square meal' ritual the cadet had to make all eating motions in a square pattern, eyes staring horizontally ahead. Not only did this make finding the plate and food difficult, but also the mouth!"

Cadets were allowed to answer officers in one of three responses: "Yes, Sir; No, Sir; No excuse, Sir." Without warning, a cadet could be commanded to "brace" anywhere, anytime until it met the satisfaction of the upperclassman. When lowerclassmen became upperclassmen, they usually took their revenge out on the poor guys just coming in and so the system was perpetuated through the war.

That actual flight training facilities were available for expansion in 1942 was another example of Hap Arnold's unorthodox way of getting things done without having the appropriations. In late 1938 it had become evident existing training facilities in the Air Corps were inadequate. Ar-

*In his article, "U.S.A.A.F. Pilot Training in World War II," HISTORICAL AVIATION ALBUM, Vol. XVI, 1980. Most of the material on the AAF pilot training system was researched through this article.

By 1940 and 1941 every National Guard unit was assigned a BC-1A—This 123rd Observation Squadron aircraft arrived at Oakland, California, in July 1941. With this model, North American had arrived at the definitive shape of their now popular trainer. *(Pete Bowers)*

The designation of NAA's product was finally changed when the BC-1A became the AT-6—the aircraft were identical in most respects. The BC-1A and early AT-6 can be readily identified by the ADF loop or football and fuel selector bubble fairing beneath the center section and the venturis mounted on the right forward side of the fuselage. This AT-6 exercises its gear over the clouds at Randolph in early 1942. *(Bamberger via Pete Bowers)*

nold called the heads of the most prominent civil flight training schools in the nation together in Washington to discuss transfer of the Primary Flight Training phase to contract schools—there was no existing money from Congress but Arnold assured the owners that would be forthcoming if they would start. A law also had to be changed that would increase the number of pilots that could be trained in non-military schools. Typical of Arnold maneuvering, the new Public Law No. 18 passed on April 3, 1939, by a bare two votes.

In May 1939 nine civilian schools were contracted to start Primary Training in July—these became known as the "nine little Randolphs," among them Rankin in Tulare, California; Cal-Aero in Chino, California; Spartan in Tulsa, Oklahoma; Parks in East St. Louis, Illinois; Boeing in Oakland, California, and Curtiss-Wright in Glendale, California. Primary lasted 12 weeks with new classes beginning every six weeks, later reduced to 10 and five in 1942. By May 1943, 56 primary civilian contract schools were operating but by 1944 they were phased out as the AAF peaked in manpower.

Primary involved such aircraft as the Boeing Stearman PT-17, Fairchild PT-19 and Ryan PT-22. Both the Stearman and the Ryan were known as difficult aircraft to master, with reputations for washing cadets out rapidly. The Fairchild, on the other hand, was quite docile and general opinion said the BT-13 and AT-6 were harder to master as a result.

If the Aviation Cadet had trained in one of the "plush" civilian schools, Basic Flight Training was a rude awakening because he was now firmly back in the military system to stay. The BT-13 and 15 (powered by 450 hp P&Ws or Wrights, respectively) were nicknamed Vibrator though Vultee preferred the given name Valiant. By 1943 it was found the Vultee did not offer enough difference from the next step up, the AT-6, so it was replaced by the "Six" with only difference between Basic and Advanced being one of curriculum.

During Basic the cadet had to demonstrate proficiency in navigation, instrument flying and aerobatics with an emphasis on coordination and smoothness. Selection for single or twin engine advanced was made at this point and students who failed were usually assigned to bombardier, navigator, gunnery or mechanical schools.

Moving on to Advanced and the AT-6 was a moment very few forgot—if one had made it that far, something very bad would have to happen to prevent earning those silver Army Air Force wings. John E. Most, Class 42-K, arrived "in the first class at Marianna, Florida, for Advanced. It was so new we used to straddle trenches for latrines. It was supposed to be a Twin Engine Advanced Training base—when we arrived the parking area was lined with single engine AT-6s. They weighed and measured us, kept the smallest guys and sent the rest to Twin Engine in Georgia. Lucky for me I stayed—I ended up commended Outstanding Student, 42-K Single Engine Advanced Continental Training Command.

"Things were rough at Marianna. Many guys ground looped. Others, to keep it straight, went off the runway into deep sand. A large number of planes were out of service—the CO raised hell and threatened severe punishment but unfortunately the only runway was in a cross wind. Still, a lot of guys made it and were graduated as fighter pilots.

"Then came orders to our first base. Fifty percent of the guys from Marianna were assigned to Twin Engine transition at Homestead, Florida, and we became Hump pilots stationed in the China-Burma-India Theater. Incidentally, one of the things I remember about the AT-6 was a game we'd play during formation flying—the wingman had to get his wing tip as close as possible to the leader's fuselage . . . between his wing and his tail . . . and not hit him."

There could be no question the AT-6 was an airplane that had to be mastered—it offered the student a challenge and it rewarded cadets as thoroughly as it punished them. Although a good acrobatic trainer, it had vicious high speed stall characteristics and when spun, it tightened up quite fast. Harold E. Scott, Class 43-B at Mather Field, California, remembers warnings against flat spins and that if one could not recover, to bail out on the inside of the spin. Many recall a student and instructor who got into a flat spin—the instructor ordered a bail out and went over the cockpit sill on the inside of the spin. Looking up, he saw the student stuck on the outside fuselage, trapped by the spinning aircraft. Laboriously, the cadet climbed back into the cockpit, then out again onto the inside and jumped. The aircraft impacted perfectly flat and crumpled into a pile of junk.

Once mastered, however, the AT-6 became the key to one's future in the AAF. Quite often students who became more than skillful in the Six were recycled straight back into the system as instructors after graduation. For those who wanted to get to fighters or other operational types, this was a blow to plans and dreams . . . to others, it was the opportunity to excel.

Bernard R. Marsh had been sent to glider pilot training just as the program was winding down and he was transferred to the Aviation Cadet program, where he went through the PT-22, BT-13 and then to Luke and the AT-6 where "my first flight was a 35-minute orientation ride on 6 November 1943. After three more dual flights, I soloed. Two months later, 7 January 1944, I graduated and after a ten-day leave returned to Luke for duty as an instructor pilot.

"The transition from student pilot to instructor pilot was indeed rapid and compressed. After six flights and thirteen hours in the back seat, I was a fully certified IP—at least on paper. My first flight as an IP involved an aerobatic check-out. I recall this flight quite well even today because when demonstrating an Immelmann, I pulled the stick back just a bit much at the top and the Six, as it was prone to do, did a beautiful half-snap. For the remainder of the flight the student was never told in advance what the maneuver was that I was demonstrating until I had successfully completed it."

All the aircraft on the line except the P-40 and the A-20s belong to the 107th Observation Squadron, Lousiana National Guard, including the BC-1A in the olive drab and gray camouflage of the era. All of the aircraft had just taken part in the joint Army/Navy maneuvers during the latter part of 1941. *(USAF)*

A BC-1A in the markings of the National Guard's 120th Observation Squadron at Biggs Field, Ft. Bliss, Texas, on October 18, 1941. *(USAF)*

A BC-1A of the 110th Observation Squadron gets a temporary water-based camouflage scheme for the Lousiana maneuvers on August 16, 1941, at Texarkana, Texas. The shades are probably Dark Green 30 and Olive Drab 31. *(USAF)*

An AT-6 of the 79th Pursuit Squadron, 20th Pursuit Group at Oakland in 1941 with a yellow cowling which had a silver leading edge. *(Bill Larkins)*

Another 20th Pursuit Group AT-6, this one with the 55th Squadron carrying a blue cowling and metal leading edge, at Oakland in June 1941. The number above the group designator on the tail meant 71st airframe in the group. *(Bowers)*

By early 1942 many of the older aircraft were repainted—this BC-1I is still serving as an instrument trainer (30 BC-1s were modified for this mission, hence the I). *(Schuler via Pete Bowers)*

Recalling the organization and flying curriculum at Luke Field, Marsh put into perspective the AAF wartime training experience . . . "The airfield proper was a macadam surfaced rectangle, unevenly split by a north-south concrete runway which we referred to as the P-40 runway. Normally, the AT-6 aircraft did not use the runway but instead used the macadam surface on either side. The take-offs for the first period in the morning and afternoon were made from east—the ramp side of the field—to west, using all the surfaced mat. Since no control was exercised over the take-offs, care had to be taken during this mass gaggle to avoid splashing aircraft over the Arizona desert. Take-offs for subsequent periods were made to the north or south on 'inside Luke'—that portion of the field nearest the flight line from the P-40 runway—and landings were made on the outside portion. Both inside and outside Luke were used for landings at the end of the final flying period in the morning and afternoon.

"The flying organization followed the traditional group-squadron arrangement; however an instructor did not follow his students through all phases of the flying training. One group was assigned the responsibility for transition, another for navigation and another for instruments. I was one of those unfortunate IPs assigned to a transition group where the really hard work was performed. We were responsible for checking the students out in the aircraft, the transition maneuvers, and a checkout in formation and aerobatics. My log reflects many entries of five, six and seven-hours days in the cockpit, and during those hot Arizona days, you could easily justify your hundred fifty per month pay. Additionally, we flew for ten days running before having one day off. We were eligible for what was called 'permissive' TDY [temporary duty] at the end of each three months. This was in reality three to five days off but not charged to leave time; however, the workload did not always permit taking advantage of this policy. Naturally, we instructors in the transition groups used to envy the easy life of those in the Nav and Instrument groups.

"The daily training schedule was not different from the one followed today—morning flying and afternoon ground school for one class; the opposite for the other, with a periodic flip-flop. Flying training began in the AT-6 'simulator'—the skeleton of a plane firmly mounted to a platform and designed so that the gear and flaps could be raised and lowered. This device served for cockpit orientation and practice with the gear and flaps, with emphasis given to attaining proficiency in making the desired 20° flaps setting without looking into the cockpit. The flying curriculum was also traditional with one exception. A selected group of students received a few hours in the P-40 and gunnery in the AT-6. The gunnery phase was accomplished at the Gila Bend base complex and included air-to-air and air-to-ground gunnery. My log shows about 30 hours devoted to this phase with 16 air-to-ground and 14 air-to-air sorties. The air-to-ground consisted of strafing only—no bombing.

AT-6s of the 83rd School Squadron on the line in 1941. *(USAF)*

AT-6s from Luke Field, Arizona, visit Moffett Field, California, on March 7, 1942; cowlings are painted red. *(Pete Bowers)*

Probably the finest film produced around the AT-6 was "I Wanted Wings," 1940. This Paramount Pictures still has a caption worth quoting in full, "The plane [Lockheed Orion] in the foreground, ready to film AT-6 training ships at Kelly Field, is flown by Paul Mantz, veteran Hollywood stunt pilot, and the sleek, shiny jobs are ready to perform for Paramount's 'I Wanted Wings,' saga of Army Air Corps training and tactics. More than $25,000,000 worth of training planes, pursuit planes and bombers form a background for thrilling action featuring Ray Milland, William Holden, Wayne Morris, Brian Donlevy, Constance Moore and Veronica Lake. Company of 130 spent a month at Randolph and Kelly Fields, near San Antonio, to get realistic backgrounds, actual conditions under which pilots train." *(Pete Bowers)*

"The basic formation flights included three-ship, six-ship and one twelve-ship flight. The navigation phase required both day and night flights and round robin as well as strange field landings. Instruments consisted of sessions in the Link Trainer and hooded flights in the bird. Of course, no fancy radio aids or flight instrumentation were available—radio range orientation and beam letdowns were just about it. Needle, ball, airspeed and the mag compass were primary in all instrument flying.

There were few examples of the AT-6 more stunning than the all-metal finished AT-6As of 1941—this one sits at Moffett in September 1941 while visiting from Stockton. *(Pete Bowers)*

This captive AT-6A at Stockton Army Air Base was used for crew training in landing gear retraction, June 1942. *(Pete Bowers)*

As World War II progressed, many AT-6s were painted in operational camouflage. This AT-6B has seen some wear while flying out of Laredo AAF, Texas. *(USAF)*

This armed, camouflaged AT-6 flies over the California coast in mid-1942. *(Harry Gann)*

"As far as flying techniques, we did not use trim for take-offs, landings or normal maneuvers. The strong right leg served as a trim tab during maneuvers at speeds lower than cruising and the left leg for speeds above. A flap setting of 20° was used for landing although settings above normal were permitted if pattern conditions required; however, it was not recommended that full flaps be used in gusty or crosswind conditions. It was standard procedure to leave the canopy open during all take-offs and landings. We taught what was called landing from the bottom of the glide. If executed properly, the glide angle would remain the same throughout the final approach to touchdown. During the landing phase, the nose of the aircraft was slowly raised until, ideally, the three-point position and stall were reached a couple of inches above the ground, and the point of contact would be the same spot as if the glide had not been broken."

Instructors and students found one of the greatest challenges while flying together was communication—even with a good intercom, it was quite easy to be thinking in two different worlds. "Just a few days after arrival for Advanced at Selma, Alabama, Class 43-I," recalled Lawrence L. Goldwasser, "and with only a few hours logged in the AT-6 and with no aerobatic time, an Air Inspector came into our ready room looking for a victim. Student officers were always fair game, and this time I was it. This lieutenant colonel wasn't very big—he must have stood on tiptoes to pass the physical—but he made up for lack of size in his attitude; he was all spit and polish, brisk, and down-to-business. Rumor had it that he was a West Point graduate.

"The plane assigned to us unfortunately had a faulty intercom—I could only catch every third or fourth word. Since the Colonel had explained what I was to do while we were still on the ground, the bad communication wasn't evident until we were up in the air. I was to break out of the pattern, climb to 5,000 feet, and start doing slow rolls. I slopped through two or three when he blew his stack in disgust. He tried to explain over the radio, and finally had to resort to hollering. He finally grabbed the controls and put us through an 8-point slow roll. He yelled back, 'Now that's the way to fly a plane!' It *was* beautiful.

"Since the intercom was so bad, there wasn't any point in staying up, so he shouted for me to take it back home. So, back to the pattern. While I was on final, I thought I sensed his feet on the pedals and his hand on the stick. 'Okay, if he wants to land, let him'—and I put my feet on the floor and my hand in my lap. We made the smoothest, sweetest landing I'd ever experienced, and as soon as we touched down, my feet and hands were back on the job. I taxied in, climbed out, and waited for the expected tongue-lashing concerning my so-called aerobatics. He didn't even look at me—but as he walked back to the ready room he was shaking his head. At last he said, 'Lieutenant (I had already earned my bars in the infantry), you can't do acrobatics for sour apples, but you can sure land an airplane!' Well, someone did, and it wasn't me—if it wasn't the Colonel, that AT-6 must have landed itself—they always said a plane flies better hands off!" Goldwasser finally mastered aerobatics, graduated to the P-47 and was shot down to spend 10 months as a POW after only 11 missions.

Landing the "Terrible Texan," as it later became known, was the most demanding aspect of flying the aircraft. Without undivided attention and quick reflexes, one could "lose" it in a split second and it would ground loop. Without hard opposite rudder, use of the brakes or a burst of throttle around it would go with results from embarrassment to a destroyed aircraft. The most common spare parts needing replacement in the AT-6/SNJ inventory were the wing tips—they were usually first to get hit. A good burst of power could pull the aircraft out of trouble in many different situations—Sidney Smith, while instructing, once had a student in the front who was excessively hard on the brakes until at one point he was about to nose the thing over on its back. Smith applied full aft stick and full power—the Six leapt off the ground and started flying again.

"In 1945," remembered Gerold E. Bickley, "I flew an AT-6 from Greenwood, Mississippi, to Dallas' Love Field. On arrival the plane suddenly started to ground loop. Fortunately, an intersection enabled me to let the thing keep going to the left. I just spun it around or let it spin around a full circle as the tower advised me that was the wrong turnoff. I maneuvered back on the runway while finally getting the bird under control at the same time responding to the tower, 'Roger, tower, I will continue on the active runway until the assigned ramp is reached.' I covered my rear end, so to speak."

As most instructors and students affirmed, flying instruments was often a mystery. When Bickley was in Advanced at Blytheville, Arkansas, he asked his instructor "to teach me how to orient myself on a radio range. We went up in the AT-6 and he maneuvered for about a half hour and gave up, saying, 'Hell, I don't know how to do it, either.' Later that year I taught myself while flying a B-25."

Although instrument flight had been perfected to some very fine tolerances by World War II, the average AAF pilot was not a part of an intensive instrument program. Kermit Mathison, Class of 43-C, "soloed the Six after a 30 minute orientation ride. Boy, what a feeling—600 plus horses, sharp rudder control, a little mushy on the stick and oh so smooth—the Six was like going to heaven without dying. In acrobatics we learned to use the wobble pump for longer inverted flight."

Mathison went on to become an instructor in BT-13s before being assigned to Bryan Field Instrument School for rated pilots in December 1944, "where our instruction was done in the AT-6. They were equipped with a full set of instruments including radio compass and ILS [instrument landing system]. The ILS unit was the only one in existence—it was highly experimental, as were many other things at Bryan. For instance, Col. John Duckworth, base CO, an old Army and airline pilot, flew a Six into the eye of a hurricane—probably the first known attempt at question answering.

"The aircraft's range with two 55 gallon wing tanks and about 25 gallon per hour fuel consumption was a little short for an instrument cross country where you had to pick an alternate field plus one hour. Therefore, Col. Duckworth, working with operations, came up with 12 P-40 wing tanks, designed a cockpit release, and mounted them between the wheels. Pronto—the only base in the AAF with 12 AT-6s with belly tanks, giving us another two hours flight time. Of course, that dropped airspeed to about 135 mph and was mushy but gave us about six hours flight time for cross country.

"Imagine tower instructions to take-off from mid-runway to the west at Biggs Field, El Paso, Texas—field elevation 4,000-plus feet—mountain off the end of the runway, with B-29s landing to the west on the same runway, on approach. I'm in a belly tank Six—when I reach the mountain I am only about 100 feet up. My only choice was a 180° diving turn and right back down the same runway at about 50 feet altitude—B-29s landing under me and the tower going wild. I gave him a wag and headed back to Bryan.

"Instructors at Bryan could clear themselves back into the field when the base was closed because the Six was equipped with ILS. In the summer of '44 a GCA [ground controlled approach] unit had been built at Chanute Field, Illinois. The unit was sent to Bryan for field testing—an operational crew came with the trailer unit. They were to use Bryan instructors for the flying and I was one of the four selected. I was then the first to receive take-off instructions so, as far as I can tell, an AT-6 shot the first GCA landing in the military. We flew the traffic pattern contact, receiving GCA instructions from the unit. In the afternoon we flew the pattern hooded with an observer.

"During the 11 months I was at Bryan I had about 800 to 900 hours in the Six. Of all the planes I flew, the Six was the most fun. She gave you the thrill of power but required the finesse of a magician to fully enjoy her."

There was, however, more to getting Army wings than learning to master the AT-6—part of what sets military flying apart is formation work. John B. McMaster, later to become an instructor himself, reminisced, "Following our initial formation flight, Lt. Joyner, my instructor, briefed us on the techniques of formation take-offs and landings, following which we got into our individual AT-6s and taxied out for take-off. The twothree ship vee take-off was accomplished without any problem. The only difference between taking off and flying straight and level formation was that one had to hastily take his hand off the throttle and, without looking down, find and pull up on the landing gear handle.

"As we approached the grassed auxiliary field, Joyner signaled for us to lower our landing gear and half flaps. I had no idea where I was, nor did the other wingmen as the secret of making successful formation landings was not to hold the same lateral position as in flight, but a vertical position which permits the lead ship and wing ships to touch the ground simultaneously. This is accomplished by having the horizon cut the exact center of the lead man's head.

"As the formation neared the ground, Joyner, of course, gradually reduced his throttle setting and we automatically did the same in order to hold position. Our first landing couldn't have been better and we took to the air to try another. Again, we approached the auxiliary field and again, we set our ships down smoothly in perfect formation. Then just as I had said to myself, 'Oh boy, this is great fun,' I must have relaxed a little for I let my little bird ground loop to the right. It whipped about two-thirds of the way around as I watched helplessly and with horror my left wing came within inches of scraping the ground. Fortunately, it didn't and as the ground loop slowed down and the wing began to come up, I completed the 360° turn and poured the throttle to my engine in an effort to get back on Joyner's wing.

"As luck would have it, Joyner had not witnessed my goof, but I hadn't quite caught up to him when he swiveled his head to the right. Seeing me lagging behind, he picked up his mike and screamed, 'Dammit McMaster, get up here where you belong.' 'Yes, Sir,' I said."

Robb R. Satterfield, flying out of Williams Field,

Arizona, in 1943 and 1944 enjoyed every minute of it—if nothing else, the ole Six was the constant source of events he would never forget. "During my days at Willie I remember one classmate and fellow instructor who, prior to a maintenance test hop, did not check his flight controls and the ailerons were somehow reversed. He did a complete roll on take-off, then chopped it and made a hard landing without too much damage. Another had the throttle linkage come loose at about 15" Hg, made it back to the field and couldn't convince the AT-6 to land. Cutting the mixture or even the mags would have helped, but he went the length of the field floating along at five feet or so and tried to go around. Got the gear up and eventually the flaps but could not climb. Took out most of the phone and power lines between there and Casa Grande and finally bellied in into an open field!

Those were certainly the days. Lt. James P. Christy (right), a former boxing champion, is teaching Cadet John "Buddy" Lewis who used to play baseball with the Washington Senators, to fly at Randolph. *(USAF)*

The major Army Air Force trainers of World War II at Tuskegee Army Air Base, Alabama, in early 1942—from back to front, the PT-17, BT-13, AT-6 and P-40. Older P-40s were used for advanced fighter transition training. *(USAF)*

A Laredo AT-6C over Texas on May 16, 1943—when flying the aircraft, it was almost always standard to keep the canopy open. It was one of the more exhilarating aspects of flying the Texan. *(USAF)*

Laredo AAF became a gunnery training center for the Army Air Force in World War II—this AT-6C comes in after a sortie on June 8, 1943. *(USAF)*

A formation flight out of Luke Field, Arizona, carrying the distinctive orange and white striped cowlings. *(USAF)*

"Another cadet was making a fast, flat let-down at night, misread his altimeter and hit the ground. The wings came off, the engine, the tail. They did not find him till mid-morning next day, hanging in his harness inside the cockpit bird cage with many broken bones. But he survived. Don't know if he ever flew again.

"For all local flying, we had a Tower Officer to handle emergencies and back up the enlisted tower personnel. It was a one-day-at-a-time rotational thing among the instructors. They were usually 1st lieutenants and not combat returnees. One day this boy captain was Tower Officer, a recent overseas returnee with many ribbons and fairly well impressed with himself. Suddenly, over the radio comes the message, 'King Uncle, King Uncle (Williams Tower)! This is York Three Four! My engine just quit! What shall I do?!' Our captain hero wades through the sergeants and corporals, grabs the mike, and says, 'York Three Four, this is *Captain* Snodgrass (your troubles are all over, I'm here). Stay calm, mister. What is your position? The cadet came back, 'King Uncle, this is York Three Four. I'm still on the ramp. I haven't taxied out yet!' At this, our captain turns instant red and tries to melt into the floor. He was a rather subdued fellow—for maybe three days."

Instructors were faced continually with long days and green students but "it was a lot of fun," said Dave Leonard, "although at the time there were occasions that flying 60 to 80 hours a month, sometimes 8 to 9 hours a day got to be tedious. Take a cadet up, shoot landings, fly-formation, teach acrobatics. Land, refuel and number two was clambering into the pit. But I'll tell you, I'd do it all over again in a minute."

Another Luke graduate and instructor, E. R. "Bob" Beard, Class 44-C, refuses "to refer to it as the SNJ. I remember the original AT-6A through D models were made with gunnery training rear seats that could swivel. That one was tough on the back seat instructor due to the low position of the seat. I can still have bad dreams about a turn to final at night with a student in the front seat. We could not see the runway lights after the turn, and the radio speaker was a hand mike, and the hydraulic system had to be activated by pushing a knob at the lower left side of the cockpit before the gear or flaps would work. So . . . you controlled the stick with your knees, tried to hold the gear handle with your left foot (cause some of them would pull the gear up instead of lowering the flaps) and still have enough hands left for the throttle and the mike to let the tower know you had to go around cause you did not know where the runway was, let alone the perimeter lights." Yes, siree, instructing was *fun*.

"Lots of cadets tried to get me," remembered W. F. "Bill" Koerschner, Jr., "but I was elusive. I remember teaching spins to a big wrestler type kid. I did one each way and then told him to try one. Went fine until the recovery—then opposite rudder—stick *full back*. Into a spin in the other direction. Talking to him, 'OK, son, let's try that again only remember to put stick forward.' Same results—he's *frozen* on the stick. By this time I try to over-power him. No go. Finally, I unbuckled my seat belt so I could raise up enough to *kick* it out of his hands. Finally recovered at 2,000 feet after losing 6,000. It seems to me that someone along the line must have shorted him on spin instruction. Needless to say, he didn't make it very much further through advanced"

Regardless of the joy of flying and the challenge of instructing, instructing was, on the whole, considered a form of punishment for those who longed for combat duty. William M. Bell* remembered a Kelly Field "instructor pilot had become fed up with his job, before he started to fly C-46s over 'The Hump' in the CBI Theater, after several requests for his transfer had been denied. He flew back to base as twilight faded into darkness and called the control tower for landing instructions. Clearance to land was issued to him over the radio, he lined up with the runway on a long, straight-in approach, turned the AT-6 upside down, and flew it to the airfield boundary. Then he turned the landing lights on, righted the plane, and touched down on a perfect three-point landing while the traffic controller's voice screamed in his earphones that he was landing upside down."

In all probability there will never be another period in aviation history like World War II. Many different facets make it unique—the sheer volume of men and machines, a spirit of unity in a common purpose, and excitement in flying the "hot ships" of the day, the thrill of learning to fly as a Cadet who wanted nothing more than to be a part of it all—who would do it all without pay if necessary. North American's AT-6 seemed to be the symbol of all that World War II aviation in America represented since it was both a hot ship and the doorway to the best aircraft flying.

No one has better summed up those days than Carroll R. "Andy" Anderson, Luke Class of 43-F who later went on to fly P-38s with the 475th Fighter Group in the Pacific . . .

---

*As told to George A. Reynolds, MILITARY JOURNAL, Vol. 2, #3, Winter 1978/79, p. 9.

"My mob arrived from Pecos AAB via a troop train ill equipped to carry anyone, let alone a large group of aviation cadets and their wives, as was the case in several instances. In fact, the trip from Pecos to Phoenix remains vivid in my mind as a trip in dirty, actually filthy cars filled with grime, loose dirt, cigarette butts and other debris. In my case, I slept on the edges of two seats back to back.

"We stopped over in El Paso for a six hour layover, and since Pete Laturno was a border kid from Harlingen, he escorted us into Juarez to a family bar where with his Spanish and our money we promptly went zonkers on the best of Mexico's tequila, which, incidentally, cost a munificent seventy five cents per bottle. The proprietor was so pleased with our presence that he gave each of us a freebie bottle upon leaving, which we proceeded to imbibe enroute to Douglas, Arizona, where the first of our contingent was let off the train. I think I only slept well from Douglas to Phoenix, and then I had to share a partially disassembled seat, made into an improvised bed, with Dusty Rhodes and his wife, who I hasten to add slept on the aisle side of the arrangement.

"At Luke, we straggled forth to be escorted to the field via GI truck, which was a conveyance designed to fracture spines and inhibit sitting as much as possible. Once on the base, we were properly impressed with the cleanliness and somewhat more permanent look of the place. Pecos AAB was black tarpaper barracks equipped with oil stoves. At least at Luke we had white barracks with some type of central heating. Within a matter of two days we were on the flight line with Group III under the command of Capt Leland Frazier, of whom we saw little. Squadron 9, of which I was a member, was commanded by a superb flier and outstanding military man, Lt Jack M. Arthaud. His right hand man was Lt Lawrence J. Pickett who eventually wrangled an overseas assignment and was killed in action.

"My instructor was a new one direct from Mather Field, named Terrien, who had developed absolutely no degree of discipline, and in fact displayed an almost total disregard for the flight rules promulgated by Capt Frazier. Terrien worked on the principle that it was necessary for the cadet to fly the AT-6 aggressively, and as a result of that immediately was in trouble.

"The procedure at Luke was quite simple. Each class took off on the mat and landed on the mat as divided by the runways which crossed the field in a gigantic X. Take-off occurred on the left side of the runway and landing was on the opposite. At Luke we flew a rather complicated box let down system, although I had no trouble with it, having experienced it at Ft. Stockton, Texas, Primary. The technique required was simply this: a cadet, ending a flight, flew out the 45° leg and after clearing the area beneath his AT-6, made a series of 90° box turns constantly losing altitude until arriving at pattern altitude. The let down was made in the direction in which the 45° leg would be flown, so that upon arriving at pattern altitude, the pilot banked onto the 45° leg, entered the downwind leg, turned on base, then turned on final.

"It was possible to view as many as 20 AT-6s, or more, descending in this manner, above and below each other, or scattered along the 45. It worked, and there were no mid-airs while I was at Luke. Although I flew the pattern well, I could not adjust my glide pattern to hit the right side of the mat, either when in close to the runway where I had the entire field before me, or on the outskirts where I had far less to hit. I constantly flew the pattern too high and even full flaps didn't help. I don't think Terrien 'pink slipped' me; apparently he saw something in my flying technique which merited holding a definitive action in abeyance.

"At the end of my third hour, I suddenly developed a feeling for that rather flat appearing glide angle and, having once instinctively registered this, I had no further trouble in hitting the first 25 percent of the mat.

"Terrien was adamant that his cadets keep their heads on a swivel. He made each of us sit in the back seat with the canopy closed to visualize the blind status of his position when instructing. We never came close to hitting anything except some yucca plants. Terrien was a man with a gifted vocabulary which he did not hesitate to use, although the tempo of his profanity was rapier-like and sarcastic rather than crude and vulgar. It seemed almost as if we were embarked at once upon violations of the USAAF rules when he took us buzzing behind the White Tank Mountains. Terrien briefed us to the effect that 'we need low altitude flying to protect ourselves in the event we became involved in combat from which escape would only occur if we flew lower than anyone else.'

"As soon as we were solo he took us buzzing in pairs, with him leading. The old rule, 'don't fly lower than me,' applied and we obeyed it. Of course, he flew about 10 feet above the ground, so it was especially difficult to get any lower than his AT-6. He told us that we were to keep our mouths shut, and if anyone said that he had authorized us to buzz, he would deny it, so away we went. The only admonition he made was, 'Don't come back with any cactus in your engine.' All of this, of course, clearly broke every rule or regulation passed by the Army Air Force.

Top
Combat veterans becoming instructors at Randolph, mid-1943. Red surrounded star and bar is just being added to the inventory and each of these AT-6Cs has wood rear fuselages and horizontal stabilizers, painted a silver dope. Total aluminum savings amounted to 200 pounds per aircraft and the wooden versions were actually heavier than their aluminum counterparts. *(USAF)*

Bottom
Randolph rat race! When the leader called for everyone to stick to him, no matter what, it was time for some unforgettable fun. The guys in the rear are starting to have some problems and the fella out to the right has been whipped out of the formation. This was part of military flying in the 1940s. *(USAF)*

Unusual mid-1943 camouflage for an AT-6-NA. In addition to red surrounded star and bar and yellow serial number on the tail, the aircraft has olive drab upper surfaces shaded with medium green around the edges and neutral gray undersurfaces which sweep up to the leading edge of the horizontal stabilizers.

With the AAF operating in all climates by 1943, a cold weather version of the AT-6 was ordered with skis and a Harvard-type exhaust heat exchanger. The type was never put into mass production and it was certainly an unusual sight in the skies over Dallas. By this time the name "Texan" was appearing in NAA and military references to the AT-6/SNJ. Since almost all AT-6s and SNJs were built in Texas during the war, the name was a natural though it did not catch on with military pilots until the late 1940s. *(USAF)*

In fact, however, the techniques he taught us did help all of us later on, overseas.

"Terrien taught us to land the airplane with our toes on the brakes. As he said, 'It's a ground looping son of a bitch.' 'Use the brakes,' he'd yell. 'Get off the God damned rudder.' 'It ground loops around 45 miles per hour, so watch the sunuvabitch.' I never came close. The wings always seemed to wobble as the T-6 slowed down, and from the high front cockpit, it seemed as if the wings were dipping very, very low. That's when we used the brakes. I had no trouble landing in the slight crosswinds we experienced at Luke. When a real crosswind developed, the pattern was changed; however, once in awhile before the pattern changed, we'd be landing five and ten airplanes across the mat in a crosswind, and it could get hairy. I once saw a cadet lose his AT-6 and veer crossways against traffic. He didn't ground loop it, and he didn't hit a single plane, but there were some real seconds of sheer panic as everyone wiggled and waggled a bit to get out of his way.

"I once was privileged to see one of the Chinese trainees land his Curtiss P-40 on the taxiway adjacent to the parking area. Somehow he became disoriented and put it down, just as a weaving class of AT-6s were working their way into the parking areas. There must have been five or six AT-6s S-ing when the P-40 touched down coming at them head-on, at about 90 miles per hour. I was told later that the tower operators were going out of their collective minds trying to get the Chinese fighter pilot to go around, this before he touched down. Story has it that he kept responding to their instructions by replying, 'Loger, loger, loger.' In any event, the AT-6s—all of them saw him coming and either dived into the parking area or plunged out onto the mat to let him get by. He managed to get it stopped and all those cadets in the AT-6s survived without a dented wingtip.

"There are those who will tell you that the AT-6 can be dangerous in a spin. Our instructions were not more than three turns, but like a number of cadets, I immediately went up to about 9,000 feet and spun it until I lost track of the turns. I even tried it with power on, and that was one thrill which amounted to 'once was enough.' The Six spun like a top, but I never had recovery troubles. I've often wondered since if the problem of spinning in an AT-6 wasn't simply panicsville and improper recovery techniques.

"Terrien taught us soft field take-offs by stomping down on the brakes, giving the engine full throttle and then letting the brakes off gradually with brake correction to keep the aircraft from swinging. I forgot how many degrees of flap he put down, but it seemed as if we were off the ground in just a few hundred feet. He used to soft field land the airplane the same way and stomp on the brakes hard enough to raise the tail and make the tires skid. His reaction to possible criticism for his instructions was that you lived if you learned to do these things, and if you didn't you'd sure as hell bust your ass some day when you shouldn't have. It seemed to work. I can't recall that any of my group of cadets was eliminated by Terrien, although he cursed a great deal on occasion.

"Night flight was dual until Terrien felt that we were competent to fly solo. One night while circling in my zone awaiting for a light and a call to come in and shoot a landing, we all received a call to return to Luke and to prepare for an immediate landing. We were brought in very rapidly one after the other and once on the ground were brought to the ready room, by jeep instead of on the elephant trains which worked the flight line day or night. Capt Frazier had everyone lined up at attention as I came in, and he wasn't polite when he racked me to attention. We just stood there, for what seemed hours, until all had been taken, individually, to his office where we were interrogated not only by him, Arthaud and Pickett, but by our instructors as well.

"Someone had buzzed a DC-3 airliner going into Phoenix SkyRanch and had been seen by everyone in the aircraft. We all were in big trouble, but since no one actually knew who had done it—the culprit wasn't about to confess—we all got off. At this late date I can say it was Max Beall from Philadelphia, Mississippi. Whether or not Max survived the war, I do not know, but we all would have gladly killed him that particular night.

"Calvin Oscar Anderson from Freewater, Oregon, my bunkmate, was the hotshot of the squadron and of Luke Field, gaining the highest air-to-air gunnery score at Ajo gunnery base. He was a fine shot and later over Leyte he bagged two Japanese fighters within a couple of minutes, one after the other, as they swept in low over the beachhead striking at our shipping and LSTs. For all practical purposes that was the only time Cal got a real chance to fire his guns, and he didn't miss. I was lucky to hit the broad side of a barn.

"The AT-6 was a dream to fly and my warmest memories of the aircraft were the light movements required to move the aircraft about the sky. It was one of the most responsive planes I ever flew, and it was ideal for formation flying. Terrien again insisted that we 'tuck in,' and on one occasion, in an effort to dramatize the point, he brought his T-6 in so close he bumped my right wing tip, deliberately. That's an experience.

"Our instrument training was done with an instrument instructor. All told we were to get six hours dual instrument and then about another six hours with a 'buddy.' Of course, we had to find ourselves in a quadrant, bracket the beam and then fly into the cone of silence before making a procedure letdown. All of this was done on the radio from Phoenix SkyRanch. The west beam had a series of false beams, so one had to make sure before bracketing. I could find myself in the quadrant and bracket any one of the beams, but in six hours of instructor dual and another six hours of 'buddy' rides, I never hit the cone of silence. If the AT-6 was good for everything else, it was lousy for instrument flying since the slightest wriggle of the stick could move the aircraft far enough to miss the cone of silence.

"I was in big trouble, and I knew it, however, since the final test flight was to have been with Terrien, I hoped for some degree of benevolent understanding. Who knows, perhaps God would look upon me with favor. Instead of simply going through the modest check, he gave me the works. I managed everything satisfactorily, even to maintaining my altitude within 50 feet. As we headed in towards the cone of silence, I was covered with sweat. The sky was smooth and we had no appreciable wind, so drift was not a problem. I had gotten through the false beams OK, and now as I headed east and the signal grew stronger, I was cutting it right down the middle, and all's I had to do was hold it steady. The one and only time I hit the cone of silence now happened, and Terrien didn't even bother to have me make a procedural let down. 'Come on out from under the hood,' he yelled, and as we flew over metropolitan Phoenix, he asked, 'Did I ever show you where my wife and I live?' When I replied in the negative, he dipped the left wing to an exact house and said, 'Right there.' This was followed by a split-S straight down, and I mean straight down, at the house, followed by a pullout that caused me to black out completely. 'Think she heard us?' he asked. Good Lord, everyone in Phoenix had heard and seen us.

"Terrien could really fly the AT-6. He used to do four point rolls and he used to yell, 'Attack,

attack! You can't do anything aerobatic by being gentle. ATTACK!'

"Night cross countries were a real experience. I had enough problems navigating in the daytime without trying it at night, but do it we did, and no one got lost. In the end I came to enjoy night flying, and I never worried about it. I also enjoyed night landings. I never worried about getting the aircraft down. If anything, I made better landings at night than during the day, although one night when we were dual, Terrien and me, we blew a tire upon landing. I managed to hold the AT-6 perfectly straight until the last possible moment when it then swerved off the runway onto the mat. I hadn't bounced it in—we simply had a bad tire, and it blew.

"The next night Lt Jack Arthaud just happened to pick me to ride with. I gave him a good flight and a fine three point landing. He allowed as how it 'wasn't bad, so let's do it again.' Three landings later, all good ones, I must have satisfied him, because he only rode with me once more and that was for my acceptance ride at the end of the course. When I finished with the AT-6 I flew the Curtiss P-40 . . . but that's another story."

Gunnery training at Tyndall Field, Florida—students in the top turret of the Lockheed Ventura track the AT-6 with gun cameras. *(USAF)*

Most of the AAF's potential gunners had to train in the AT-6. This flight from Harlingen, Texas, prepares to do some work near the Gulf of Mexico. *(USAF)*

A target sleeve is released by an AT-6 after a gunnery mission—note the bumper around the tail wheel to prevent fouling. *(USAF)*

Air-to-ground gunnery, Luke Field, March 17, 1942. The major problem with teaching gunnery was not the popping of the .30 caliber in the cowling, but the tendency to fly into the target. Yet, as the AAF caption to this photo said then, "the cadet becomes a regular 'Dead Eye Dick' with this modern weapon, ready to deal death to our enemies and glory to himself." *(USAF)*

Once the AT-6 was mastered, pilots found transition into the operational types a natural step up into a very similar aircraft. The cockpits of the AT-6 and the P-51 were comfortingly alike. Though the fighters of the day were a challenge to land, they were no more squirrelly than the ole Six. The instructor's manual used through the life of the aircraft summarized it well, as quoted here in the 1948 Air Training Command BASIC FLYING manual:*

Landing Planning

The T-6 has seven characteristics that affect the performance during the execution of a landing, they are:

1) A tail wheel lock will desengage readily if the tail oleo strut is inflated too high or if the tail wheel is turned in excess of 15° from the centerline of the AT-6D aircraft. Worn tail wheel locking pins can shimmy, causing confusion to pilots unaccustomed to it.

2) Lack of sufficient rudder trim to maintain a coordinated power-off glide (even with full left trim). Therefore, it is necessary to hold a little left rudder.

3) An appreciable torque effect if power is applied abruptly, in a great amount, and at low airspeed.

4) A pronounced tendency to 'weather vane' into the wind after landing cross wind.

5) Noticeable ground effect (buoyancy) when landed with full flaps and slightly excessive airspeed.

6) Frequently worn and/or maladjusted oleo struts that often cause one strut to stick down upon ground contact.

7) A fairly high center of gravity compared to the distance between the wheels. This condition is conducive to a lateral instability in ground turns. Furthermore, this condition is intensified by a low oleo strut.

As with the SNJ, the AT-6 found many tasks assigned to it that had departed from the training mission. Pilots earned flight pay or maintained currency in the Six, even in the B-29 training program. Chester Marshall recalled that it played an important role "during the summer of 1943 while B-29 crews were assembling at their bases in Kansas—major problems popped up everywhere. Delivery of the bug-bitten B-29s was slow and it became a constant hassle for some crew members to get a meager four hours flying time per month in order to draw flight pay. To solve this problem they brought in AT-6s, B-17s and other type aircraft.

"In this role the Six was to play a larger role later on and I was a part of it. After completing 30 combat missions against Japan in B-29s, I was rotated back to the States in July 1945. My new assignment was flight instructor at Roswell AAB, New Mexico. Hostilities had ceased, of course, and over 4,000 officers—pilots, navigators, etc.—receiving training there were left with nothing to do since flight training halted.

*Provided by former T-6 instructor Sidney E. Smith.

"Again, there was the problem of these men losing their flight pay. And again, the AT-6 was brought in. Instructors were ordered to take a 'passenger' up, fly three hours and shoot 10 landings in order to qualify him for 'four hours' flying time and his flight pay. You should have seen the giant traffic pattern around Roswell Field in those days. This job eventually got boring, but I never lost the thrill of flying the wonderful AT-6."

Not only was the aircraft used Stateside, but it appeared in large numbers in every combat theater during World War II. Some were normal AT-6s but AT-16s, the AT-6A built by Noorduyn in Canada under lend-lease, and Harvards found their way into USAAF service, some bearing their original RAF serial numbers. Again, they were used for currency or in getting bomber pilots transitioned into fighters. Every AAF fighter group overseas was authorized to have two AT-6s for instrument training and general hack flying.

Bob Moore, who served as crew chief on the two AT-6s used by the 404th Fighter Group, 9th Air Force in Europe, was only 18 years old at the time. Operating the aircraft from their headquarters at Straubing, Germany, the 404th P-47 drivers would fly instrument qualification and VIP transportation missions in the colorful birds. Bob recalled the brakes never seemed to be adjusted and he enjoyed watching the pilots land it—always interesting since the P-47 was easier to handle. He was continually installing new wing tips but he thought it was better duty than working on the P-47s since it was a much simpler machine. There were a total of three with one used for spares. Pilots would often get lost, landing in Czechoslovakia, only 15 miles away.

A great deal of use was made of AT-6s and Harvards by the 8th Air Force in England as the following documents recount:

SECRET
HEADQUARTERS
ARMY AIR FORCE STATION F-342

6 December 1943

SUBJECT: Harvard II B Aircraft

TO: Commanding General, VIII Fighter Command

1. There are four (4) Miles Masters, MK III, two (2) Miles Masters MK II, and two (2) Harvard II aircraft on this station Atcham, Shrewsbury for use in P-47 transition training and instrument and flight checks. The difficulties and delays encountered in securing spare parts for the Miles Master types make them less desirable than the Harvard type aircraft from a maintenance view point. The fact that the instruments, brakes, control columns and general cockpit layout are quite different on the Miles Master from those encountered in any American aircraft, renders the Miles Master aircraft practically, although not completely, useless in P-47 transition training and as flight check aircraft.

2. In the interest of safety, it is believed advisable to require newly arrived pilots, with some exceptions, to demonstrate their proficiency in an aircraft of the Harvard class rather than permit them to make their first flight in England or their first flight in an American airplane in an aircraft of the P-47 class. The availability of only two Harvards at this station has at times in the past proved a bottleneck in the rapid, efficient and complete processing of pilots to assignment to operational groups.

Lt. Col. Robert W. Humphreys, commander at Atcham, the 8th's fighter transition base, went on to request eight Harvard IIBs from the pool at Speke Aerodrome at Liverpool since there were about 52 in storage there awaiting assignment. Some went to the Royal Navy and others to the Russians but the request was turned down on the basis that all the Harvards had already been assigned.

Above
The AT-6 was also prone to flipping over on its back if things got too far out of hand, as this bird demonstrates at Rosecrans Field, St. Joseph, Missouri, on April 18, 1945. *(USAF)*

Opposite page top to bottom
The cockpit of a BC-1A, 39-831, which set the pattern for most AT-6s and SNJs that came after. The bulky radio compass controls are in the lower center—oxygen controls are on the lower right and the pointed selector dial on the left cockpit side turns the venturis on or off for powering the vacuum instruments. *(USAF)*

The cockpit of the last AT-6 to be built in the NAA Inglewood plant. 41-665 was an AT-6A-NA while 41-666 was an AT-6A-NT, a Dallas-built bird. *(Dusty Carter/AAHS)*

SPARE LAMPS
IGNITION
RADIO COMPASS
VOLTS
AMPS

ARM REST

By 26 May 1944 the situation was bad enough to force Col William G. Lee, Jr., to write the following from Cheddington:

CONFIDENTIAL
HEADQUARTERS
VIII AIR FORCE COMPOSITE COMMAND
ARMY AIR FORCE STATION AAF - 113

26 May 1944

SUBJECT: Request for AT-6 Aircraft
TO: Commanding General, Eighth Air Force

Replacement pilots now arriving at fighter CCRC's have logged an average total of eleven (11) hours of instrument time, actual and 'under the hood'. This is less instrument time than the minimum required a short time ago for graduation from flying school. In view of the exceptionally unstable and hazardous weather encountered in this theater, combined with the extreme tactical necessity for operating during conditions of solid overcast and low visibility, it is vitally necessary that these replacement pilots receive at least a dual flight check, and, if possible, additional dual instruction before being scheduled for 'cloud flying' in single-seater tactical type aircraft.

The four (4) AT-6 aircraft now assigned this command are located at AAF Station 342, the P-47 CCRC, and are being used to accomplish the dual instrument checks and instruction summarized above. Of the eight (8) additional AT-6 aircraft requested [by Col Humphreys], four are urgently needed to supply similar facilities for the P-51 and P-38 CCRC at AAF Station 345 [Goxhill, Lincolnshire].

Four (4) stations of this command, in addition to the fighter CCRC's are in the peculiar position of having assigned to them a number of single-engine or dual-engine pilots, but possess no single-engine or dual-engine planes in which 'under the hood' instruction checks can be accomplished. As a result, the instrument currency of the rated pilot personnel, contrary to the provisions of AAF Regulation 50-3, has of necessity lapsed with no early prospect of renewal unless an American two-seater dual control aircraft can be provided at those stations. In addition to the requirements for an instrument check plane, these same stations lack any communication type aircraft which can be safely cleared for necessary liaison flights during instrument conditions.

When the total of AT-6s was tallied in mid-1944 it came to 23: seven each in the three air divisions, one each in the Headquarters Flight of the Eighth Air Force and VIII Fighter Command. By this time the Atcham and Goxhill fighter training centers had been dissolved and each fighter group had to train its own replacement pilots in "clobber colleges", resulting in the following HQ 8th AF request: "there are at present twenty-three (23) AT-6 and AT-16 aircraft assigned to this Air Force. US Strategic Air Forces in Europe Memorandum 65-2, 31 January 1944, authorizes each group using fighter type aircraft one (1) dual place instrument training aircraft. There are seventeen (17) operational units of this Air Force authorized this type aircraft." Before the year was out, the AT-6 was a common sight on most fighter bases and many bomber bases in the ETO, each aircraft bearing the markings of the particular group.

With the end of World War II, many types were surplused or sent to the smelters, including the AT-6. On the whole, however, the Texan, as it was slowly becoming known, escaped this fate due to its usefulness. It was chosen as the main aircraft for those in the Reserves to fly, then it was phased into the Air National Guard. By 1947 the AAF was turned loose and the United States Air Force was born as a separate service. By 1948 designations changed on certain aircraft as pursuit was changed to fighter (the P-51 became the F-51) and the prefix letters were dropped from trainers. The AT-6 became the T-6.

With thousands of wartime pilots flooding the Reserve and the ANG, the T-6 was often the only aircraft to fly, regardless of what type the pilot was flying before. Getting bomber pilots qualified in the Six was often a hair raising proposition. Walt Allen was one of the "lucky" ones to fly with these pilots as he logged time in the AAF, Reserves and ANG . . . "I had several interesting experiences flying with rated pilots who had never flown the AT-6 or had been away from the airplane for several years. I found that some pilots who had been through multiengine advanced training found the AT-6 to be quite a handful on landing.

"Except for the fact that you could not fully operate from the back seat, I found it to be fun and a challenge to fly from the hole in the back. It was not possible to raise the gear from the back, although you could lower it. To fly from the back you sort of had to develop eyeballs in the side of your head. I blew a prop seal one day and there was oil all over the place. It was the first ride for the pilot in the front seat so I landed from the back without difficulty. What the hell, you couldn't see anything even when there was no oil on the windshield.

"The other joy in the back seat was the heat or lack thereof. By the time the hot air got to the exit to the heater duct it was lukewarm. We were flying the T-6 in Vermont and Maine in the mid-

With the end of World War II, thousands of pilots were let out of the AAF but aircraft were painted with the slogan, "Enlist in the AAF—Guard the Victory," as this AT-6 at Randolph shows. *(USAF)*

Buzz job! This AT-6F at Coraopolis AAB, Pennsylvania, March 10, 1946, carries a belly tank modification for extra range, normally for extended instrument time aloft. *(Balogh via Dave Menard)*

dle of the winter and I spent many chilly hours shivering through a flight. In the summertime we used to fly around with shirtsleeves rolled up and the canopy open. This would probably cause the safety experts to have fits these days but we were young and having fun.

"We did learn to close the canopy if we were doing acrobatics because when the engine backfired it could send a sheet of flame down the side of the fuselage which could burn if the airflow was just right.

"One day while doing a spin the mechanical uplock on the gear released and the gear swung down. The spin tightened up and the centrifugal force knocked my feet off the rudder pedals. It really took a tremendous effort to get the feet back on the rudder pedals so that I could stop the spin. One night I tried a barrel roll using some small Texas town for orientation. I lost the town and for a few hairy seconds I did not know which way was up. That was the last time I tried a barrel roll at night when the sky was as black as the ground and there was only one small patch of lights for orientation."

By the time the USAF put together a post-war flying training program, it was realized the T-6 was once again vitally needed. When the Class of 48-B arrived, the first Cadets since World War II, Primary Flight Training was made up of ½ Stearmans and ½ T-6s. With 48-C the Stearman was gone and students started out in the Six with zero flight time. There were doubts about such a hot ship being suitable for the job but, just as the Navy had put the SNJ with its primary students, the Air Force went ahead and tried. It worked but later the system was changed and the Piper PA-18 Super Cub was used to introduce Cadets to flying before going on to the T-6.

Al K. McDonald, who had been flying P-61 Black Widows, was one of those who was recycled back into instructing with the new influx of cadets . . . "I left to instruct at Randolph during the big cold war buildup. Quite a switch from flying the P-61. I'm not sure if I started with the first or second class to start in the T-6. Prior to this they received Primary Training in Stearmans.

"We had four students per instructor and flew

Two WASPs (Womens Airforce Service Pilots) get ready to take-off on a target towing mission from Camp Davis, North Carolina. Those Santiago blue uniforms were stunning, particularly to the guys who flew with the WASPs. *(USAF)*

three dual flights per day. As I recall, the students had to solo within 20 hours of dual time. Of course, flying that regular we got pretty sharp in that back seat. The worst thing they would do to you is get sick and try to puke over the side which immediately flew back inside the plane. We used to make them unzip their flying suits and puke inside them, then zip them up. Immediately upon landing they hit the showers flying suit and all!

"The interesting times included acrobatics in the hot Texas summer. Three flights a day would really do it. Even a simple loop the first few times would end up with pencils, bugs, dirt flying around as they pushed the stick the wrong way on top. We gave them a little dual formation, then with the instructor dual in the lead and a solo student on each wing, off we'd go. After a couple of hours in the air it would be time for their first formation take-off on the runway at the west stage. I'd brief them to line up, run the engine up with brakes on and when I nodded my head, we'd all release our brakes and take-off together. I still wouldn't trust them at this period so I'd release my brakes, start rolling, *then* nod my head. This little head start would get me out of the way in case they ground looped.

"Instructing Primary/Basic students wasn't the best duty at that time for a fighter pilot. However, it was one of the few assignments where you could see the results of your efforts in a short time. When we'd be flying formation I'd look out on each wing and realize I had taught that kid to fly. Great feeling!"

Al vividly recalls making the great graduation formation fly-bys that characterized flight training during that era. "The take-off for the big fly-by was on the runway, west stage. The main air show was on the east side but I think we had more spectators on our side. We took off in letter formation (masses of T-6s would spell out classes and words). Since our flight was the eighth to take-off, prop wash was already bad. It got worse as the whole flight started rolling. The worst part was just after the wheels left the ground and before you could drop below the aircraft in front of you.

"All the pilots were instructors and had a lot of T-6 flying. The rest was a piece of cake. We landed in an echelon on the grass on the west side."

Avenger Field, Sweetwater, Texas—this woman is in the process of earning her wings as a WASP with the AT-6. WASPs flew every major combat type in the AAF. *(Norm Avery)*

Cadets in these first classes, including Doc Blanchard in 48-C, went from the T-6 into F-51s, B-25s or B-17s depending upon what branch they would ultimately serve in. By 1949 it became evident the T-6 would have to be modified if it was to meet the growing needs of the USAF. In a study of 173 T-6 ground loop accidents, recommendations were made for a new type brake lining, better cockpit seat adjustment and installation of an F-51 type tailwheel lock/steering system.

The Air Force took a hard look at the problem and decided to order remanufactured airframes under the designation T-6G, starting in 1949. NAA eventually rebuilt 2,068 Texans which it had to get from civil owners as well as what was available in the military inventory. After the war the AAF had no idea it would end up buying back its own aircraft. Pete Vandersluis, who later became an instructor, recalled the U.S. government offering $8,000 to anyone with a T-6 or SNJ in 1950 and 1951 as the program gathered steam, ferriable to Columbus, Ohio, where they were gutted and rebuilt.

The rear seat was jacked up six inches, the canopy frame cleaned up, an F-51 tailwheel system was installed (forward stick for full swivel, back stick for rudder pedal steering), updated radios and instrument panels installed, no power push for the hydraulic system but automatic activation with the gear or flap handles, no hydraulic pump in the cockpit, modified wings with 30 gallons more fuel due to two bladder tanks. The extra fuel not only made it a longer legged cross country aircraft but an instructor could spend an hour each with four different students before having to refuel.

New NA charge numbers were assigned to the aircraft, which also bore new USAF serial numbers—the old serial numbers were then stamped on the turnover bar so that one could keep track of the original airframe. NAA's Downey, California, plant remanufactured 641 airframes for the USAF and another 50 for the Air National Guard, as well as 50 LT-6Gs as Forward Air Control aircraft in Korea—these were labeled NA-168s. The Columbus plant rebuilt 824 for the USAF, including some T-6Fs that were temporarily redesignated T-6Hs—these were NA-182s. NA-188s came out of Long Beach, California, 107 for the USAF but all were assigned to the Mutual Defense Aid Program as T-6Gs for foreign governments. The 11 T-6Gs remanufactured at Fresno, California, as NA-195s were assigned to MD Aid as well, while the other 110 Fresno airframes came out as NA-197. The only other variant was the T-6J, covered under NA-186—these were the 285 Canadian Car and Foundry-built Harvard Mk. IVs which were purchased under USAF serial numbers for MD Aid—though some ended up as USAF aircraft, most were delivered to Belgium, France, West Germany, Italy and Portugal.

With a great influx of remanufactured Texans, the Air Force was once again a beehive of training activity. Most of the USAF's pilots who were trained between 1948 and 1955 would well remember the T-6 as the first military airplane they had ever flown—even the first they had flown period. Jack Gale, Class of 51-G, got his first taste of flying in the PA-18 before going on to "the Big Yellow Bird, as we called the Six, because, simply enough, it was painted that color. We put 120 hours in the Six, broken down by phases

The sole XAT-6E, an AT-6D modified with a 575hp Ranger V-770-9 engine. It was 30 mph faster but Pratt & Whitney reliability was too good to give up. *(Harry Gann)*

and training requirements. No one, except for those who pose for mental health posters, would ever say that the 13 hours of instrument time required in the rear seat of a Six was enjoyable. And, very seriously, I am sure that the vast majority of those who washed out of Primary Flight Training did so because of difficulties with the instrument phase, or the carryover effect of the fear of being totally shrouded in the canvas bag covering, which was your 'under the hood' instrument intro and indoctrination.

"We were taught almost totally by a civilian contractor that supplied the flight and most of the ground instructors. We flew our mandatory check-rides, and non-sched rides with Air Force IPs, but they came in only two categories—damn good or damnably young and lacking in empathy.

"The Six in no way prepared you for the T-28, which was the first plane in Basic Flight Training. The '28' had an almost identically arranged cockpit configuration to the next step, the 'T-Bird' [T-33] . . . but I still say the hours alone in the 'Yellow-Bird' were sheer and total ecstasy. Considering the total 260 training hours spent in all four aircraft prior to graduation, the T-6 was really relaxed fun."

As sophisticated as the Air Force was supposed to be getting with the jet age, hard helmets and G-suits, Cadets continued to sit in the dark ages during Primary. Allan L. "Bud" Young, Class 53-D, went through Primary at Bainbridge Air Base, Georgia, from late April to December 1952—"almost everybody that completed the course there did so with one to three flying hours left over that they had to fly to complete flight hour requirements even though the training requirements had already been met. This meant that for one or more flights the completing student was told to go fly with no specific mission assigned.

"It was on one of these flights that I was assigned a brand new T-6G that only had about nine hours total time. I reasoned that since this was not an old, tired trainer it would be capable of climbing to a relatively high altitude (where I had never been before), so off I went to see just how high it would go.

"After climbing for close of one hour with the throttle beyond the sea level stop and pushed hard against the forward stop on the quadrant, mixture properly leaned way back and prop still at climb rpm, this new 'Terrible Six George' was lazily chugging along at 24,500 feet with only 15" of manifold pressure showing on the gauge, while I enjoyed a most spectacular view of the Georgia countryside and could faintly discern the landwater contrast of the Gulf of Mexico—far to the south.

"Here I must mention that even though many of us would be going on to jet fighters and even sooner to the T-33 while still in training, none of our schooling to date had approached any aspect of the physiological effects of a lack of oxygen on the body although I do remember some hanger flying bull sessions that rumored something about an 'altitude sickness' that could occur at 'higher' altitudes. Additionally, whether from our instructors or other bull sessions, we had been told that the most rapid altitude loss maneuver was a spin, in deference to a high speed spiral, since the steady state spin generated relatively low stresses on the airframe and the rate of descent was relatively high.

"So, while enjoying my lofty view and mentally boasting of the extreme height I had obtained, my elated spirits were dampened by an increasing headache and a stomach sickness that I couldn't at first explain. Momentarily, the 'altitude sickness' story came to mind, followed immediately by the rapid descent cure analysis followed by the rapid descent means—the now familiar spin. The rest was easy since our standard spin entry procedure consisted of lowered air-speed, throttle 15″ Hg, stick back and boot respective rudder for a left or right spin—then just hold everything until recovery. I say the rest was easy for I had most all prospin conditions set up long before as a result of high altitude. So—an inch or two farther back on the stick to the aft stop and boot in the left rudder—left only because I preferred left spins.

"Just as advertised! Break, left wing drop, nose rises a little and normal rotation is established. I believe I felt better already! After three or four turns of a blurred world, I decided possibly I should count the number of turns—no reason—just count 'em—so as the sun rotated about me I counted.

"Gradually it seemed as though the spin rate was increasing and I noticed that the manifold pressure was no longer the desired 15″ but was up around 24″! Throttle reduction brought it back to 15 and the spin rate reduced to about normal. As I passed 10,000 feet on the altimeter I began to think about what altitude I should terminate the spin and decided that 5,000 feet would be a good round number where there should be sufficient oxygen and also altitude for recovery of both cadet and machine.

"This plan was immediately junked shortly after my sun counting peripheral vision caught sight of two or three other T-6s rapidly moving straight up rather close by as I realized I was spinning down through the transition training area—

"Having just said 35 to myself I popped the stick forward, booted right rudder and was out of it—the harsh environment and the spin something below 7,000 feet—and headed the hell out of the transition area (and all those nasty instructors) with an amazingly rapidly recovered head and stomach ache.

"The remaining 15 minutes of my flying period were spent in gentle descending turns towards the landing pattern. In summary—I doubt that 24,500 feet is anything unusual for the T-6 unless it be at the hands of a 150 hour cadet. More unusual perhaps was the near 40 turn spin that brought that same cadet safely back from the then inner fringes of space."

Thomas Dorsey, Class 53-B at Goodfellow AFB, Texas, had a hard time getting used to the military system—every five demerits a cadet had to "walk a tour" with full military dress and assorted accessories; Dorsey got 21 demerits, but thought the chow was served in the finest mess he could recall during his long Air Force career. At Goodfellow the standard 360° overhead approach was made over the northwest runway in Phase I of Basic, which started zero time students in the T-6. One cadet came in and pitched out right—when this was done, much rudder was required, especially if power was needed on the final turn, or the Texan would snap and spin. This guy did a fine one turn spin over the mobile control unit and just pulled out. It took two hours to talk him back in to land. Other students were killed by this same mistake.

Dorsey recalled many of his class having to stay with the T-6 for the rest of Basic when others went on to the T-28. He thought the Texan drivers were better off in the long run, even though they were often treated by the T-28 guys as lowly types. But Dorsey was convinced one could get sloppy in the T-28—never in the T-6, which *made* one fly.

By the time the USAF training program gathered steam again in the early 1950s, a great deal of the flight training was once more contracted out to civilian firms. Pete Vandersluis was hired at Greenville, Mississippi, at a contract primary school as a civilian instructor. Though 19 years old, he looked 15 and the interviewers doubted he could fly, but he was hired after 1.5 hours of split-S-ing out of most of the maneuvers he was required to do without ever having had aerobatic training. After some dual to show what the Air Force required in the way of instruction, he was sent to Craig AFB, Alabama, in February 1953, then Selma flying T-6Cs, Ds and Gs.

Of the 150 students in the class, 75 were American and 75 were French sergeants who would all become instructors. Pete promptly set an example by doing an aerobatic show for his girl friend. Entering a loop at 120 knots, he forgot to push the hydraulic power push when trying to use flaps over the top and went into an inverted spin at 8,500 feet. Too low to split-S out, he recovered and pulled out inverted at 1,200 feet. The Frenchman in the back said, "That was neat, let's do it again!"

All versions of the NAA trainer saw extensive overseas service. This French NA-57 (BT-9B) has been pressed back into AAF service on reverse lend-lease for use by the 90th Photographic Reconnaissance Wing in North Africa, late 1942. *(USAF)*

Pete went on to instruct at Marianna, Florida, then joined the USAF and went through training on proficiency before getting his wings in B-25s. He then went straight back to instructing in T-6Gs at Malden Air Base, Missouri. On January 13, 1955, he gave his first check ride in the Air Force—"The first student I had got on the wobble pump and the primer, then backfired the engine which caught fire. Every time he would hit the primer and the wobble pump, the flames went higher around the cowl and I was yelling at him to stop priming. I opened the throttle and tried to pull the mixture into idle cut-off. Of course with the lock on the mixture [in the front cockpit], I couldn't do it and I'm yelling at him to pull the mixture to idle cut-off.

"The flames really started spreading so about then I yelled, 'Get out!,' turned off everything, threw my shoulder harness and seat belt off, left my chute on and jumped out. As I jumped up on the step, the shoulder harness caught in my parachute and my foot came off the step—I came down on the canopy rail you know where, went headfirst over and hung with my head about a foot from the ground upside down by my shoulder harness.

"It wasn't more than a few seconds I was covered with foam from head to toe from the fire truck. That was my first check ride. The student was so rattled he failed and washed out."

Vandersluis remembers the majority of the students as quite enthusiastic and capable, giving a minimum of four check rides a day. After 25 hours in the Super Cub, if a cadet did not solo the T-6 in 18 hours he was washed out. The initial program was 140 hours in the T-6, then 120 and finally 110 after the Cub. Most of the horrors, however, of flight training did not involve flying—out of 24 cadet deaths, 18 resulted from car wrecks.

Pete made his last USAF T-6 flight on December 14, 1955, with the Class of 56-Q as the Texan program was winding down. The T-6s were gradually flown to Arizona where they were surplused, stored or scrapped. The Venezuelans flew many of the Texans away—37 pilots showed up and when the leader gave the signal, all 37 fired up and took off at once! When they landed in a buzzing gaggle at the base south, a national alert was triggered because none of them talked on the radio.

Engines were normally changed at 2,000 hours. Out of 110 aircraft, the average daily availability was 90 while the T-28 averaged 40 to 60 per day out of 160. As a result, the T-28 drastically hurt contract primary flying schools. Vandersluis* believes the T-6 would have saved more lives by washing more cadets out than the T-28 did but the need to simulate the jets made the T-28's career. Ironically, the rebuilt T-6G owes its life to the many bugs that had to be ironed out of the T-28, causing its delayed entry into the USAF inventory.

*Pete Vandersluis now owns and flies a T-6G painted in the markings of one of the aircraft he flew in the 1950s.

An AT-6 attached to the 33rd Pursuit in Iceland and Greenland, surrounded by ice and snow. The red stripes have not been painted on the rudder. *(Kay Bettin)*

This AT-6 at Charleroi, Belgium, in October 1944 was painted with black and white invasion stripes. Every fighter group in Europe was authorized to have an AT-6 as a trainer and proficiency aircraft, usually painted in the distinctive markings of each group. *(Fred LePage via Fred Johnsen)*

AT-6s attached to the 404th Fighter Group, 9th Air Force at Straubing, Germany. The red-yellow-red fuselage bands indicated U.S. occupation force aircraft based in Europe after the surrender while the yellow spinners, cowling and lightning stripe down the fuselage were unique 404th markings. Note the wheel hub decorations. *(Arthur Houston)*

Capt. Miller with one of the 404th Fighter Group's AT-6Fs, decorated by yellow spinner, cowling and fuselage lightning stripe and red-yellow-red fuselage bands. 404th AT-6 crew chief Bob Moore took care of the birds while they were used for instrument training and P-47 checkout preparation. *(Arthur Houston)*

Though the Piper Cub was utilized as a Primary trainer by the Air Force, cadets continued to be placed straight off in the T-6 and it was an awe inspiring experience. Vernon D. "Bud" Hesterman was in Class 53-F which began with the T-6 . . . "To me, as a young Kansas farm kid with no previous flight experience, the T-6 was one hell of a big and awesome machine. Even the starting and taxiing procedures were scary and complicated. I recall my civilian contract instructor saying that taxiing should be easy for me because it was just like driving a tractor on the farm. He was wrong on that particular point but the rest of his instruction must have been effective as he eventually told me he was tired of having me try to make his wife a widow and if I wanted to fly the airplane, I'd have to do it myself.

"What a glorious feeling that came on that marvelous day when I turned out of traffic and realized for the first time that I was actually flying a big, beautiful, powerful airplane all by myself. There may be greater life experiences than that first solo in a T-6 but, offhand, I can think of none. I had long had the idea that pilots were right up there next to God and at that moment, I knew for sure they were."

Charlie Weidinger recalled a classic instructor/cadet story from his days at Malden in 1953:

IP: 'Remember, don't *ever* let me catch you using that wobble pump before starting the engine! You can start a fire under the nose! Just give 'er two or three good shots with the primer. Now, let's get this thing started!'

CADET: 'Yes, Sir!' (While vigorously nodding head up and down in Pavlovian agreement).

1. Cadet unlocks primer, pulls handle slowly to rear to get a good fill, then presses handle firmly downward to prime engine. (Of course the IP cannot see this action).
2. On second fill, Cadet yells, 'Contact' and Fireguard looks away, supremely bored.
3. With primer full a third time, Cadet presses down with heel on starter pedal to spin up flywheel, switches mag switch to BOTH, and while mashing toe down on starter pedal to engage starter, notes distracting motion on left side of seat near landing gear handle.
4. Cadet notes that handle of wobble pump is merrily bobbing fore and aft. Meanwhile, starter engages, engine starts turning, and Cadet remembers to press and lock primer.
5. Soft, explosive 'thumps' from somewhere forward of windscreen do not sound proper to Cadet, who also notes large quantity of white smoke curling up around engine cowling.
6. As frightened Cadet goes through emergency stop procedure, now *very* interested Fireguard is fumbling with extinguisher (a type he's never used before) as bonfire is seen licking up around exhaust stack.
7. Unstrapping, IP assumes meanest look, and yells . . . 'See? That's what happens when you use the pump and the primer at the same time! Just remember that!'

CADET: No comment.

The T-6 continued to teach its riders in ways they did not expect. As R. R. "Bob" Mottern, Class 55-E at Marianna, recalled, "reflecting back, I realize that the T-6 was such an honest airplane that it was an instructor as well as a trainer." When Bob arrived as an ROTC second lieuten-

Opposite page top to bottom

A Noorduyn-built AT-16 in service with the 89th Fighter Squadron, a P-47 outfit, at Tinghawk SaKan in the China-Burma-India Theater, December 1944, carrying RAF paint and markings. *(Ken Sumney)*

Another AT-16 at Barrackpore, Calcutta, India, on August 22, 1945, repainted as an AT-6. The black antiglare panel paint extends back across the canopy frame. *(Pete Bowers)*

This stock AT-6F served at Barrackpore during the same time period in company with the P-38s in the background. *(Pete Bowers)*

692

481923

ant, his assigned instructor was "Bob Conn from Hattiesburg, Mississippi, and since I was from upstate New York, we had somewhat of a communication problem, especially on the intercom. His favorite word was damn pronounced 'day-um' and he used it often and indiscriminately. When I did something right, he 'day-umed.' Conversely, I got a 'day-um' when I messed up."

Mottern seemed to lack the ability to wait in trying things that he had read up on further in the manual. His first loop, without ever having one demonstrated to him, was done solo—going straight up he ran out of airspeed and reacted by pulling power off. Instead of the throttle, he grabbed the prop control, yanking it back—"the racket of that error got my attention about the same time my body rose against the seat belt and my unprotected head hit the canopy." He returned to base with very timid, almost wings level turns.

A few days later, after practicing loops with Conn, "my confidence had returned to just short of the 'cocky' level." Dreaming of becoming a fighter pilot and "since I was still reading ahead in the manual and the daily thrill of flying the Six had suppressed the memory of my uncompleted first loop, I was considering the joys of that old standard, the barrel roll." Bob got half way around and relaxed left pressure to continue . . . "my mishap with the loop didn't provide me with any insight to my present predicament. For one thing when the loop went astray my frantic search for the ground revealed only sky. Now half way through the barrel roll my frantic eyes found only ground."

Bob Split-Sed with full power, thinking "back stick pressure had always brought me out of spins, loops and stalls, so back pressure it was." Once again he limped back to base. As he got more proficient, Bob learned aerobatics. While practicing half rolls with reverses back to straight and level to perfect the nose not yawing off center, "it occurred to me that if I practiced with the canopy open I too could feel the nuances of the air flow past my cheeks—Conn had extolled the virtues of open cockpit flight in the Stearman. He claimed that one could sense stalls and yaws and all manner of uncoordination from the slight differences in air pressure the pilot felt on his cheeks.

"I opened the canopy, felt the air rushing past and with great anticipation rolled inverted with supurb coordination. I held the point fine and began the reverse. Unfortunately, as I started my roll I added too much right rudder and pulled the nose off the point. The expected nuance of air never came to my right cheek. Instead I got hit with a blast of red hot, oily exhaust gas that nearly took my earphones off. I was sure that I was scarred for life. Since I was not right side up there was nothing left to be done except to shout a loud 'day-um' that Bob Conn would have been proud of. . . . I was more than a little angry at the Six for the lesson. After all, burning the side of my face seemed to be an overly harsh reprimand."

By the mid-1950s the USAF was ready to get rid of its Texans but those who were still being trained by them considered the Terrible Texan with love and respect. Richard G. Woodhull, Jr., Class 57-B at Stallings Air Base, North Carolina, remembers getting quite cocky after his first few solos—marching down the flight line in formation, his class would sing this ditty to the tune of "My Bonnie Lies Over the Ocean":

The Tee-ee Six Gee is Our Airplane,
Constructed of Metal and Tin,
A Top Speed of Over One Hundred,
The Plane With a Built-in Head-wind!
(refrain)
Gear Up, Flaps Down,
The Heck with the Instructor,
We're Back on the Ground!

This cockiness transferred into Woodhull refusing to allow a fellow student to help him strap down the back seat for a solo flight after his friend taxied in and turned the aircraft over to him . . . "I refused his offer with a rather cavalier comment about my ability and desire to do it all by myself. I secured all of the aforementioned straps, switches, etc., and got in the front seat, started the engine and taxied out for my solo flight. My attitude as I taxied out might be described as very confident, just short of smug. Moments after I became airborne, even before the gear handle had been placed in the 'up' position, I knew that something was very, very wrong. Air was rushing up into my eyes from the floor of the airplane, along with assorted bits of grass and dirt, and the slipstream around the open cockpit was rushing straight into the cockpit, buffeting my helmet-clad head so badly that I could hardly see and clawing at my helmet and sunglasses. In about 1½ seconds, time enough to swallow once and see myself walking out the Main Gate as a civilian, I knew what was wrong—I had failed to close the rear canopy! Mobile Control 'invited' me to land at about the same moment that I had figured out what I had (not) done. Beyond the embarrassment, there were no further repercussions."

Standard practice at Stallings was to fly with the canopy open at all times below 3,000 feet,

Headquarters 5th Air Force AT-6F at Nielson Field, Manila, Philippines, in August 1945. The author's father, Walt Ohlrich, Sr., stands in the cockpit of the P-40N in the background *(Walt Ohlrich)*

even in the winter—cadets were issued heavy flying jackets and the old B-17 crew wool-lined "booties." "Duke" Woodhull will never forget "one night, a dual ship (T-6 with student and instructor) broke in on tower frequency with a declaration of an Emergency and request for immediate landing clearance. The instructor was doing the talking on the radio, and he advised the tower that he suspected an imminent structural failure of the aft section or tail assembly of his aircraft. At the very same moment, the interphone conversation between the student and instructor sounded like this (later reconstructed):

Student: Sir, sir . . . what's the matter?

IP: I have it . . . relax, everything's going to be OK . . . don't panic . . . just let me handle everything!

Student: But, Sir! I . . .

IP: As you were, Mister! Just keep us clear from other aircraft . . . we're making a straight-in to 23!

"After an uneventful landing, subsequent investigation revealed that the student, who was in the rear cockpit for an instrument period, had been suffering badly from the cold. His feet had nearly gone numb, so he had been pounding and stomping them on the metal tracks or flooring of the T-6, to keep the circulation going. His IP couldn't see anything in the dark, so simply assumed that something had 'come loose.'

"Incidentally, about nine years later I was undergoing transition training in SAC's U-2 high altitude reconnaissance aircraft. The big challenge in those days was to safely land the U-2, but I had no problem at all. Why? Because landing the early model U-2s was exactly like landing a T-6G from the back seat!"

During this time period, the USAF was training many foreign students for friendly countries, as has been mentioned. Frank E. Barry had a Belgian student who simply should never have been sent to advanced training in the T-6. This student would snap the stick straight back about 15 feet over the runway and round out—with Barry board and fighting the result, the Belgian crashed the ole Texan by going into a 90° arc to the right after the right wing dropped—the nose went down and the aircraft skidded along on the prop and cowling before wiping out the gear.

Barry recalled some T-6s with three seats, the middle one for a psychologist to study instructor/student relationship and instructor methods—needless to say, the arrangement did not last long. Only the very brave would ride with green students and yelling instructors.

As in World War II, the T-6 found itself forced into other roles than training men to fly. Eugene W. Gauch, Jr., who had instructed at Randolph in T-6s, later found himself in SAC (Strategic Air Command) flying the T-6 under that awesome banner . . . "During the late '40s, SAC experienced an unprecedented number of heavy bomber (B-29s, B-50s and B-36s) incidents and accidents. The ensuing safety investigation and analysis revealed the possibility that some of the pilots may have forgotten the fundamentals of flying when making an approach for landing under less than routine conditions. It was also thought that under some emergencies, the pilot of a heavy bomber might not readily recognize an approach to a stall in a turn with asymmetri-

Sgt. Paul F. Brown teaches mechanics in China with the help of the AT-16 (42-697) in the background. *(USAF)*

The Russian lend-lease field at Abadan, Iran, full of A-20s, P-40s, a P-39 and AT-6s. One percent of the aircraft delivered to Russia were AT-6s. *(USAF)*

The other major Russian lend-lease field was Ladd, Alaska, where two Russians prepare to ferry at AT-6F back home. *(USAF)*

The war is over and these AT-6Cs have been assigned to the 473rd AAF Base Unit, Miami, Florida, to prepare Reserve pilots to get into the P-51, November 8, 1946. The AT-6 would become an important tool for the thousands of pilots who needed to maintain proficiency in the post-war wind down. *(USAF)*

Lt Robert S. Fitzgerald (lead) and Lt William J. Fenton were two Air Force Reserve pilots on extended active duty who did air shows as the "Mitchel Pair" from Mitchel AFB, New York, seen here in 1948 getting ready to perform in the Cleveland Air Races. *(USAF)*

cal engine power. Therefore, General Curtis LeMay directed that a trial program be established at Roswell AFB, New Mexico, where heavy bomber pilots would be reindoctrinated in the basic skills of flying in the T-6 aircraft.

"In March 1950, along with a handful of former T-6 instructor pilots, I was recertified as an instructor pilot at Randolph and returned to Roswell to fly with the bomber pilots assigned to the 509th Bomb Wing. During April and May of 1950 we flew daily with the 509th pilots and tried to qualify them in the T-6. If I recall correctly, the main problem we encountered was to prevent the pilots from rounding out too high on their approach to a landing and not to quit flying after the wheels touched the runway. It appeared that both tendencies were caused by many hours experience in aircraft with very high cockpits and equipped with tricycle landing gear."

It seemed there was always a T-6 around to provide some vital hack flying. Andy Henry once "had a 'personal' T-6 assigned to me on Taiwan, which enabled me to commute to various jobs around the island in my capacity as F-86 instructor to Chiang's Air Force. It was an adventure . . . no radios, no tach, trim worked backwards. Like that."

Though versions of North American's far flung

trainer saw some action on a piecemeal basis, primarily in the air forces of foreign countries, nothing has ever topped what the USAF did with the T-6 during the Korean War. For three years, the LT-6G and some of its older brothers were made Forward Air Control (FAC) aircraft to direct fighter strikes in support of ground forces, under some of the most hostile conditions military pilots have encountered.

Williams AFB, Arizona, on November 12, 1951—the T-6 was still a very important training tool. *(USAF)*

In the early '50s the next step after the T-6 was the T-33, the jet trainer version of the F-80 shown here with a Williams AFB Texan. Delay of the T-28 into the training system made the T-6 that much more important during the period. *(USAF)*

T-6Ds in 1953. A quick glance for an ADF "football" on top of the rear fuselage could usually tell an instrument trainer from a regular T-6. The instructor in the rear of the lead T-6 seems to be taking his job very seriously. *(Pete Bowers via Jim Sullivan)*

As the Korean War heated up in mid-1950, one of the primary problems was effective use of jet fighter-bombers, at that time primarily the Lockheed F-80C, which had loiter times of only 10 to 15 minutes, far less than propeller-driven aircraft. Lt Col Stanley P. Latiolais, Fifth Air Force Operations, suggested the T-6 might serve through Eighth Army Air Liaison Officer, Lt Col John McGinn as a FAC aircraft.

Lt Col J. R. Murphy and Maj E. J. Lynch asked for support from USAF Maj Gen Earl E. Partridge in getting an operations officer and five pilots for the mission. Three L-5Gs showed up with bad generators on July 9, 1950, and the first try at a mission was aborted.

Bill Mann, who had worked on the AT-6As and BC-1As at Maxwell in 1941, was in the 35th Maintenance Squadron in Korea at the time — the unit had a single T-6C which had been out of commission for over a year after an accident. As Bill recalled, "We had most of the parts but had given it a low priority due to work on the F-51s and F-80Cs. One day General Earl Partridge, Commander of the Fifth Air Force, taxied his F-51 up in front of our hangar and got out, walking straight to the T-6. He asked for the maintenance officer and told him he had one week to have the T-6 in commission. That's all he said, turning to walk back to his aircraft.

"I got the project along with the people—we got an OK flight on the first test hop five days later. After that the T-6 got a fighter priority due to their need in Korea as spotters."

Lts Bryan and Mitchell, who had flown in the L-5Gs, in the meantime flew the first FAC missions directing F-80s in the 24th Infantry Division L-17s. The next day the restored T-6C arrived at Taejon and "worked" a flight of Australian F-51s with Bryant and Mitchell aboard—the radio failed in the middle of the mission. Later in the day the two lieutenants directed F-80s onto 42 tanks and the final tally was 17 destroyed—the worth of the T-6 in combat was proven in a single day.

More T-6Ds and Fs were assigned to the mission but North American was asked to build some of the T-6Gs coming out of the Downey plant as LT-6Gs, specifically modified to serve in Korea. The aircraft had radios that could communicate with all units flying in Korea, racks for a dozen 2.5-inch white phosphorous rockets with cockpit selector box, and a single .30 caliber forward firing gun. Fifty-nine were initially delivered and another 39 were converted before the specialized version was stopped.

By July 13, 1950, the unit was established under Maj Merrill H. Carlton at K-2 airfield, Taegu, attached to the 51st Provisional Fighter Squad-

ANG
285857
WASH
ANG

ANG
012-90
CALIF
ANG

Opposite page top to bottom

By 1953 T-6s could be seen for the most part painted all yellow. This T-6D was attached to the 116th Squadron, Washington Air National Guard as a major general's personal aircraft (note two star placard below rear hood). *(Ellensburg via Pete Bowers)*

In the early '50s a completely remanufactured version of the T-6 began to show up in training units and elsewhere. This T-6G was attached to the California Air National Guard in August 1951. *(Balogh via Dave Menard)*

T-6s brace a TRF-51D of the Illinois Air National Guard. *(Dick Stouffer via EAA)*

Above top

Several T-6s served with the North Dakota Air National Guard, which flew F-51s for quite some time. An F-84 and a Mooney Mite can also be seen in this hanger shot. *(NDANG via Dick Phillips)*

Above bottom

170th fighter Squadron, Illinois ANG, T-6D from Springfield carrying the unit badge on the side. *(Dave Menard)*

ron. The older T-6s were hard to maintain since none of the LT-6Gs were on the scene and the unit only got hand-me-downs from the 51st. Nevertheless, in July 1950 269 missions were flown (as many as 29 per day) for the loss two Texans. By July 15 the nameless unit was given a series of callsigns that would be a trademark through the "police action" in Korea. A frag order that day designated missions from "Mosquito Able" through "Mosquito How" and the term stuck. Some sources credit the North Koreans with the nickname due to the sting that came behind the buzzing of the T-6's propeller.

By August 1 the Fifth Air Force got around to designating the unit as the 6147th Tactical Control Squadron (Airborne) at Taegu. Once the daring of the pilots and their observers spread, they were admired as undertaking "the most dangerous of any aviation activity in Korea." Gen Partridge assigned himself to the unit for awhile, flying combat with his second lieutenants. By the end of the month, with less than three weeks of actual flying, of the 55 pilots on the Squadron roster, 17 had already completed a normal tour of 50 missions—two crews were lost. By the end of the second month, the Mosquitoes counted 183 tanks, 119 trucks, and 778 other vehicles (not including 15 oxcarts) damaged or destroyed.

Lt Jim Brockmyer, who designed the squadron patch of a mosquito with headphones and mike directing three F-80s, wrote the following song to the tune of "Galway Bay":

Oh they say the T-6 wasn't made for combat
And I am here to tell you that is so
But I'll fly another mission in the morning
Although I'm not convinced that I ought to go.
All ye pilots gather 'round to hear my story
Do not talk of jets and Baker 29s
For this evening we'll observe one minute's silence
In memory of "Mosquitoes" on the line.

Although at 50 missions pilots were allowed to rotate to Japan for non-combat duty or to fighter units of their choice, many elected to stay for another 50. By September 1950 the 6147th was thrown into every imaginable aerial job—pursuing retreating troops, dropping leaflets, deep penetrations, search and rescue, night direction for B-26s, drop mission coordination and artillery adjustment.

When the North Koreans retreated farther north, targets became harder for the T-6s to reach so a 56 gallon belly tank modification was rigged. This gave an extra two hours cruising time but the squadron was still moved to North Korean territory to fly out of K-24, Pyongyang East Airfield, and the frigid Siberian air. In October the unit began using smoke grenades and flares in addition to radio description to mark targets.

Col Carlton, after the initial success of the smoke marking, suggested a small smoke rocket be mounted on rails under the wings—he proved his own idea by getting 76 2.36-inch rockets and tested them incountry. The first combat target marking rocket mission was flown by Lt Bruce Iverson—no fighters had to destroy the North Korean Army self-propelled gun because a direct hit with the tiny rockets knocked it out! A pilot could now fire from 1,000 feet out and then break to clear most of the murderous ground fire.

Moving back to Seoul, K-16, the 6147th was used increasingly, gaining a reputation that caused one pilot to say, "Ask any fighting GI what Air Force plane he remembers best. Ten to one he'll say the T-6 Mosquito." On December 14, 1950, the squadron put up an incredible 25 T-6s at once but the availability was reflected in hardly any T-6 coming back to base without holes and bullets lodged in the aircraft. As Maj Tim Cline* recorded, "Hostile ground fire squeezed the safe altitudes for FAC operations into a narrow band between 1,200 feet (the effective altitude for small arms fire) and 3,000 feet (where 20 mm and 40 mm anti-aircraft guns were most effective and at which height too little detail could be observed on the ground). Still the pilots pressed to get lower where the enemy could be flushed out if necessary. One Mosquito followed a set of tank tracks at altitudes as low as 10 feet, and discovered five tanks dug into a mountainside"—they were destroyed by fighters.

By January 22, 1951, the unit's 20,000th combat hour was flown by Lt James R. Topping and SFC Fred C. Heider. The squadron had flown 1,174 sorties with an average sortie time of 2 hours 45 minutes and 23 aircraft had been lost in 6½ months of combat flying.

A C-47 nicknamed "Mosquito Mellow" joined the 6147th as a "mother ship" to relay VHF radio transmissions and to serve as a senior control platform, the forerunner of command and control aircraft. Tactics were firm by March 1951—a Mosquito orbited in a left-hand turn to rendezvous near the target with the assigned fighters. Once the fighters spotted the T-6, they went to a common frequency and got informa-

---

*"Forward Air Control in the Korean War," AMERICAN AVIATION HISTORICAL SOCIETY JOURNAL, Vol. 21, No 4 (Winter 1976), pp 257-262

This T-6D and T-6F were some of the first Texans to be attached to the 6147th Tactical Control Group in Korea as Forward Air Control (FAC) aircraft. The Mosquitoes, as they became known, flew combat in the T-6 during the entire Korean War. *(USAF)*

August 1951—by this time the early T-6s were becoming pretty beat up flying with the 6147th. Note the white phosphorous rockets mounted beneath the wings. *(USAF)*

tion on the target from the FAC. The fighters would then string out in trail as the T-6 marked the target with smoke, then pulled off to circle. The fighter leader then flew in from Point A to Point B, where he started to roll in with a clearance from the Mosquito.

On March 28, 1951, Col Merrill Carlton, who was largely responsible for the 6147th's success, was replaced by Lt Col Timothy F. O'Keefe and the squadron was expanded into the 6147th Tactical Control Group, with two squadrons of LT-6Gs, the 6147th and 6149th TCS, to do the flying, and the 6150th to support ground operations. The Mosquitoes were then moved to the closest USAF base to the front, K-47, Ch'unch'on.

As the Korean War settled into a long slogging match, pilots came through the 6147th in ever increasing numbers to fly the mission. Some were extremely frustrated at not getting fighters and considered the assignment a demotion. Others flew more than one tour, like Robert N. Anderson who managed 102, although he said that someone lost count and he flew until they stopped him.

Seoul, Korea, in October 1952. All but two of the T-6s on the line were used for insect spraying, with spraying pods and checkered cowlings. As the remanufactured LT-6Gs arrived to fly combat with the 6147th, the older T-6s were turned over to other units for non-combat duty. *(USAF)*

Capt George W. Cochran checks the damage to the left wing of his T-6 after bringing back his wounded observer despite trim tabs shot away and a jammed landing gear handle, October 1952. *(USAF)*

6147th crew chief Cpl Herbert E. Powell has his work cut out for him—his T-6D Mosquito got its tail shot up while marking targets. *(USAF)*

One of the replacement pilots who came into the unit during the fall of 1952, Gene Risedorph, recalled,* "All the replacement pilots had previous T-6 time, logged during flying training days. Most of us had close-support experience, some in P-51s, some in F-80s, the author in F-84s. The training period was therefore shortened and consisted of a couple of re-familiarization rides to get the feel of the T-6 again, followed by one ride where we learned the technique of achieving accuracy with the 2.5″ rockets using a rock in a nearby reservoir as a target and a rivet on the cowling for a sight. An experienced Mosquito pilot or observer then accompanied us on a couple of trips to the front where we were coached on procedures while directing actual strikes. From this point we were considered fully qualified and placed on the regular mission schedule."

Missions were set up so that at least one T-6 was in each Army Corps area on station during daylight hours. Using terrain features initially, the Mosquito would guide fighters into the target area, mark the target with smoke, then get out of the way to watch the bombing and give a score. Risedorph continued, "We used a scoring system based on the percentage of ordnance in the target area and percentage of ordnance effective. A perfect score was '100 and 100.' A typical score would be '90 and 80' which meant that 90 percent of the ordnance hit the defined target area and that 80 percent of the ordnance was effective.

"The approach of a T-6 signaled the Communist troops in an area that an air strike was likely. After the target was marked enemy soldiers on adjoining hills would sometimes leave the protection of their bunkers and congregate where they could watch the airstrike on their comrades. Lt Ronald Ingraham of the 6149th TCS marked a cluster of bunkers on one hill, then observed a large group of Chinese gathering on the adjoining hill to watch the airstrike. The terrain was distinctive enough so that Ingraham was able to verbally describe the location of the exposed troops without firing another marking rocket. The fighters then dropped their ordnance on the 'audience' with devastating results. Needless to say, the airstrike watching ceased for some time afterwards.

"The T-6 provided a number of unusual combat experiences. Lt Dan Shipley had his rockets ignited on the racks by ground fire. The resulting hole was large enough for Shipley to stand in, but the T-6 proved sturdy enough to be patched together to fly again. Lt Dick Meade was bounced by a Yak-9 over the lines. The two aircraft flew a tightening Lufbery circle with the T-6 finally pulling lead on the Yak. Meade salvoed his rockets at the NKAF fighter and while he scored no hits, the Red pilot discovered the Mosquito

*"Mosquito," AMERICAN AVIATION HISTORICAL SOCIETY JOURNAL, Vol. 24, No. 1 (Spring 1979), pp. 45-51.

Above
Francis N. "Curly" Satterlee gets ready to fly a mission in his LT-6G with observer Peter Tolputt from the British Army. *(F. N. Satterlee)*

Below
LT-6Gs of the 6147th in revetments, March 9, 1953—many of the aircraft have their engines running and it was common to have 25 aircraft on station at one time waiting for fighters. *(USAF)*

Opposite page top to bottom
LT-6G outbound for a target over Korea, loaded with white phosphorous rockets. Some of the pilots liked to get sewer lids to sit on for extra armor protection of their more vital areas. *(F. N. Satterlee)*

With several rockets already fired, this 6147th LT-6G continues to cruise for possible target marking. *(F. N. Satterlee)*

TA-540

U.S. AIR FORCE
93-573
LTA-573

could sting and he broke off immediately heading north with great haste. An intelligence report during the fall of 1952 stated that the enemy was operating a captured L-19 in Turkish markings. We frustrated fighter pilots bounced every L-19 in sight hoping to luck on the right one. Meade's experience with the Yak-9 nurtured the urge to score a kill in the T-6. No T-6 over encountered the enemy L-19 but we did cause some concern among Army and Marine L-19 crews along the front.

"The necessity of operating at low altitude led many T-6 pilots to take the precaution of flying with the canopy open in order to save time should a jump become necessary. Hopefully a stricken aircraft would be able to climb to a safe altitude for bailout if it were hit during a low pass. Lt Tom Napier's T-6 was hit in just this way and burst into flame. Both canopies were open and Napier was able to pull up and roll the aircraft on its back allowing him and the observer to drop out. They both touched ground in no-man's land seconds after their chutes blossomed. Napier told the author his most vivid recollection of the incident was pausing before rolling the T-6, removing his headset, and hanging it on the rear-view mirror (a common practice after parking an aircraft)."

The T-6s often followed the river valley at low altitude to get home in bad weather—"it was a strange feeling," said Risedorph, "flying low along the river with the ceiling below the mountaintops on each side. In some spots the passage was only a football field's length in width. The enemy knew of the river route too, and although it ran on our side of the line all the way, guerrillas would occasionally stretch cables across the flight path. Lt Jack Pate saw a cable just in time to duck under it. He lost the tip of his rudder but made it home safely."

When the Mosquitoes started using the forward-firing .30 caliber, it did not take long for many of them to launch out on their own personal wars, taking on antiaircraft batteries and trying to kill T-34 tanks. Before he left, Col Carlton ordered the guns removed. "Your function," his order read, "is to seek out and mark targets—not fight the Communists with a pea shooter."

Before too long, other C-47s served in the command and control function as "Mosquito Shirley" and "Mosquito Godfrey." On the whole, Mosquito crews found it easier to work with the propeller driven F-51s, F4U Corsairs and AD Skyraiders due to longer loiter times and less difference in speeds. Risedorph recalled hunting for targets with two ADs on each wing and one in the slot—the T-6 was firewalled while the ADs had their dive brakes out.

Robert Anderson is congratulated by Maj Bradley on the former's 102nd mission—someone lost count and Anderson flew too many before he was told it was time to quit. Flying combat in the Texan was certainly an unforeseen event when the aircraft started to serve in the Army Air Corps but on it soldiered until the late 1950s, forever remembered by those who flew it. *(F. N. Satterlee)*

Lt Chester L. Brown flew the last Mosquito mission of the war from K-47, number 40,354! Before too long, the FAC mission disappeared from the military thinkers and the lessons would have to be learned all over again in Vietnam.

"Deep inside each T-6 pilot," reminisced Gene Risedorph, "was a frustration in not being able to deliver the heavy blow on the target. The Mosquito had to be content to watch while others conducted the actual destruction of the enemy. The frustration of the fighter pilot plying his trade in a T-6 is best illustrated by a radio conversation between a Mosquito pilot and a Navy flight leader over the front. The Navy pilot had not worked with a Mosquito before and was attempting to establish visual contact. The question was asked, 'Mosquito Postcard, I'm not sure I have you in sight. What type aircraft are you flying?' There was a thoughtful pause, then the answer, 'An F-6!' "

On September 17, 1956, the U.S. Air Force retired its last T-6 at Bartow AFB, Florida. For almost 20 years North American's wonderful Texan had trained countless U.S. military pilots. Most were not sad to see it go since old aircraft rarely get much thought when shiny new ones appear on the ramp, but to others it epitomized military flying. When Gerold Bickley was scheduled to leave the Air Force, "I checked out a T-6 at Offutt AFB, Nebraska, through an old friend for one last flight. I took the T-6 up and, sometimes through tears at the thought of a last flight, did every acrobatic maneuver I knew. It was a beautiful day and no traffic. What a lovely airplane!"

Chapter Four

Flight Lieutenants and Harvards

With North American Aviation's very successful overseas export program, founded upon the many variations of the NA-16 design, it did not take long for Harvards, AT-6s and later SNJs to find their way into an ever increasing number of air arms outside the United States. Countries that could not spend a great deal of money on sophisticated aircraft found the North American product ideal for training their pilots to fly modern military machines.

By far the largest customer for the aircraft was Britain's Royal Air Force. Once the Harvard program got underway at Inglewood (see Chapter 1), rapid expansion of the Empire Air Training Scheme was undertaken. By late 1939 the English decided to locate the majority of air training in North America, both in the U.S. and Canada. No longer were Harvards crated and shipped to England—they were flown directly to the bases using the aircraft. This created somewhat of a problem between the U.S. and Canada due to the U.S. Neutrality Act which prohibited the flying of military aircraft to a warring power. In June 1940 the first of the new batch of Harvards was flown to the Canadian border, put down on a nearby field, then pushed across the border so that RAF pilots could fly the aircraft off to its destination. This ridiculous process went on until the U.S. State Department decided it was not practical to carry on this legalistic practice and then the Harvards were flown directly to their bases in Canada.

The 1,000th Harvard came off the line in California on March 18, 1941, and it was the 570th example flown directly to Canada.

Initially deliveries of the aircraft to South America were made by shipping them in crates, but in the summer of 1938 Peruvian pilots made the first NAA delivery flight to Lima, led by Col Armando Revoredo. The first large batch of aircraft to be flown to South America were NA-44s for the Brazilian Air Force, the first six of three groups of six getting airborne on the 10,000 mile flight to Rio de Janeiro on September 11, 1940. Brazil became a prime customer for the AT-6 subsequently.

Under lend-lease, around 2,300 AT-6s were eventually supplied to Britain, the Soviet Union, China, Holland, Venezuela, New Zealand, Canada's RCAF, and many other countries. To the Royal Air Force, the AT-6C became known as the Harvard IIA while the AT-6D and SNJ-5 became the Harvard III—all of these various models of the same aircraft came off the production line together.

From the very beginnings of the aircraft's history, other nations were not only interested in buying the aircraft, but in building it in their own factories. When Australia bought the rights to build the NA-33 as the Wirraway (see Chapter 1), NAA opened the doors to others. When Canada began receiving Harvards, they chose the AT-6A for license production by Noorduyn Aviation Ltd and a first contract for 100 was placed in January 1940. In all, 210 aircraft were delivered as Harvards IIBs. The program was successful enough to have the U.S. government order 1,500 for supply to the RAF under lend-lease, complete with USAAF serial numbers, designated as AT-16s. Another 900 were ordered for the RAF, bringing the total Noorduyn run to 2,610 Harvard IIBs.

A second Canadian production effort was started in 1951 as the RCAF ordered a new production run of Harvards similar to the rebuilt T-6G. The Canadian Car and Foundry factory in Montreal, which had taken over from Noorduyn in 1946, proceeded to build brand new airframes as Harvard IVs. The RCAF bought 270 and another 285 were purchased by the USAF as T-6Js for use in the Mutual Defense Aid Program. Six of the Harvard IVs went to the USAF to replace six AT-6Ds lost in a batch of 100 on loan to the RCAF from 1951 to 1954.

The Japanese Navy evaluated the NA-37 and NA-47 as the KXA1 and KXA2 and in 1941 had their first example built and flying as the K1OW1 with a Nakajima 600 hp Kotobuki 2 Kai engine. After 26 were built, production was turned over to Nippon Hikoki KK, which built another 150 as the K5Y1 in 1943 and 1944: Of all the oddities of war, North American's trainer being built in Japan during World War II—it even had the Allied code name Oak.

The Swedish were one of the first at North American's door in 1937 to build the NA-16 after getting two specimens, the NA-31 and NA-38 powered by Wright R-975-E3s. The Swedish Air Force placed an order for 35 in July 1938, going into service as Sk 14s from May 1939 on. A second batch of 18 was built by Saab and yet another batch of 23 through June 1942. All of the Sk 14s were basically BT-9s. Later the Swedish bought 145 AT-16s as Sk 16As, 112 T-6s as Sk 16Bs and six SNJ-2s as Sk 16Cs.

2501

KDA
1182

Opposite page top to bottom
On November 17, 1939, the RAF ordered the Harvard II, which was virtually identical to the AT-6-NA. This is the first of 600 built. *(Norm Avery)*

Once the Empire Air Training Program was underway in full swing, most of the training was done in North America. Here a British Cadet readies himself for a flight at BFTS, Tyrral, Texas.

Harvard II production at Inglewood. *(Norm Avery)*

When Britain found itself pressed against the wall in 1940, it reached out to those nations who would support the war effort. Neutral nations had to take particular care in their dealings with Britain but it was no secret that the United States was going to do everything in its power to help. The major American contributions lay in lend-lease equipment that could be supplied from factories and in training bases that could be located within the continental U.S. By 1941 RAF pilots were pouring into the country to learn to fly on American soil. Former Flight Lieutenant Geoff Hirons well remembered those days . . .

"When, in its second year of war in 1941, Britain found itself lacking in facilities to train an ever-increasing number of pilots on and over its own terrain, the safe skies of Canada and the U.S.A. provided a welcome answer to the problem. The great exhibition site in Toronto provided the chief assembly point for would-be pilots from Britain and from some German-occupied countries of Europe, notably Poland and Czechoslovakia. Those destined for training in Canada departed from Toronto in the full glory of their RAF uniforms while those of us who were to bring joy to the south and west of the U.S.A. went through a process of being civilianised in order to preserve the facade of strict neutrality which the U.S.A. publically professed at that time.

"This process involved the storing of all RAF uniform and equipment and the donning of what the authorities described as: 'dress, civilian, airmen for the use of'—a description which I fear lost something in its translation to English by its unfortunate wearers. Each person so equipped was issued with a brown fibre suitcase to contain the extra clothing, tins of boot polish, etc. which were soon to impress the natives of such far-flung corners of the continent as Macon, Georgia; Phoenix, Arizona, and Arcadia, Florida.

"At some time in their glorious history of Empire making, the British must have been blessed by someone (could it have been Queen Victoria herself?) who deemed that anyone departing our island shores for parts lying between the 30th Parallels, north and south of the Equator, should at all times carry a topée (sun helmet) to ward off the rays of the sun which had caused the stunted development of mind and body of all living in those latitudes. In accordance with regulations, therefore, those destined for Florida had the addition of a topée to their equipment. To make the whole civilianising process absolutely authentic so as to completely fool the German

It seems everyone tried to get the aircraft on skis—here is a Harvard I with non-retractable skis and cold weather shutters. *(DiIonardo via Pete Bowers)*

N7018
N7140

AJ987

Opposite page top to bottom
Harvard MK-1s formate over the English countryside early in the war. The fabric covered fuselage is quite noticeable. *(Charles Braun)*

Harvard IIs on the NAA line at Inglewood. U.S. national insignia have been applied to the wings for an unusual mixture of national markings before the aircraft was delivered to the RCAF in Canada. *(Pete Bowers)*

Below
These RCAF Harvard crashes in 1943 and 1944 well illustrates what could happen when the aircraft got away from the pilot. *(R. W. Swift)*

Intelligence Branch, all prospective trainees were interviewed by staff of the American Immigration Department who ask the usual—'Name? Nationality? Sex?' (to which the stock answer was, 'Yes, please.'). Eventually we were issued with a finger-and-thumb printed Alien Registration Card.

"My own destination was to have been No. 5 British Flying Training School (B.F.T.S.), Clewiston, Florida, but either the train was faster than had been calculated or the alligators less inclined to move than had been anticipated, for in the event Clewiston was not ready to receive us and we were diverted to Arcadia. Already at Arcadia were two other flying schools—one for the US Army Air Corps and the other for the RAF using all the facilities of the Air Corps.

"Our arrival introduced a new element for while we used the Air Corps Stearman PT-17 aircraft and were subject to Air Corps discipline on the base, all our instructors were those civilians who had been engaged for our training at Clewiston. One didn't have to be hyper-sensitive to detect a certain animosity between the two sets of instructors, Air Corps and civilian. The feeling soon manifested itself in a way that affected the trainees—a 'going solo norm' emerged with up to six hours being good and anything over seven hours being sneered at (and how I hated being sneered at!).

" 'Wash-outs' (from memory) ran at 40% plus and a very nervy time was had by all. The Primary Training course of 5 B.F.T.S. at Arcadia started in July 1941 and was almost at an end when, on September 25, Clewiston was pronounced ready and we moved in. The field was designated Riddle Field and was the base of the Riddle-MacKay Aero College. The end of Primary Training and the beginning of Basic Training occurred in the middle of October, and with it a change from the Stearman to the Vultee BT-13A, a monoplane with fixed undercarriage but having landing flaps.

"After an uneventful Basic Training, Advanced Training on the AT-6A followed and was just as ordinary. I seem to remember someone saying, when the first of the AT-6As appeared in the circuit, that some poor devil's wheels had dropped off—suggesting that our aircraft recognition at that time was so poor that an AT-6A with its wheels retracted looked like a Vultee minus its undercarriage."

Geoff Hirons did not see the aircraft again after training until he was in Egypt in July 1944 fighting a war . . . "I had done a tour on Hurricanes in North Africa and a tour on Kittyhawks in Italy when someone decided I ought to have a rest. What happened next wasn't exactly restful. First I went to Ballah where I flew Lysanders, towing targets for trigger-happy air-gunners to pot at, alternating this with making mock attacks with Harvards on ancient Ansons for the gunners to pot at with camera guns.

"When the total number of holes in the rear ends of the Lysanders started to exceed those I suffered in the desert and Italy, I decided I'd had enough and took myself off down the Canal (Suez) to Fayid and No. 73 Operational Training Unit where I was training youngsters just prior to their joining Kittyhawk squadrons. As with many such units in those days there always seemed to be plenty of 'spare' aircraft around and one of ours was a Harvard. Its chief use was as a cab to return visitors to Cairo or Alexandria. There was never any shortage of volunteers for this exercise as the lucky pilot was assured of a day away from the base to enjoy the restaurants and places of entertainment of one or other of those cities.

"These flights were usually 'laid on' by the C.O. and often over a drink in the mess in the evening. The routine for offering lifts to non-flying types started with the offer and the grateful acceptance of the 'victim.' The next step was for the C.O. to look around the mess and then say, 'Smith, would you like to take our visitor back to Alex. in the morning?' After that had

A French AT-6 bellies in at Casablanca, 1951. Forgetting one's landing gear appears to be a problem regardless of who flies the airplane. *(Harry Gann)*

A beautifully camouflaged Harvard II in the Mediterranean Theater, 1944.

The Australian license-built version of the BC-1, called the Wirraway, saw combat in World War II as a fighter and one is credited with downing a Japanese Zero. Note the twin forward firing cowl guns and the flexible rear gun.

One of the many French A.F. T-6s sits in the ramp at Casablanca in 1952. Soon the training paint schemes gave way to wartime squadron markings as the Algerian was escalated. *(Harry Gann)*

been settled and the visitor had beamed all over his face at the prospect of a 40 minute flight instead of several hours in a red-hot train came the blood congealing, face whitening follow-up—'Let's see now, you've never flown the Harvard (or Fairchild or whatever) have you Smith? Better take that and see if you can get it there and back in one piece.'

"I don't know whether our base was considered a high priority for missionary work, but certainly we seemed to have more than our share of visiting chaplains and so it was that these unfortunate gentlemen took the brunt of this ploy. The Harvard was particularly suited to this exercise as a bit of juggling with the pitch control during the flight could suggest all sorts of impending disasters. An over-shoot and a bit of 'upping and downing' just before touch-down completed the illusion and, in the case of chaplains, strengthened the passenger's belief in the power of prayer."

One of those serving as an instructor with the RCAF during World War II was George B. Collinge, who flew everything in the inventory except the Norseman and early helicopters. "Other than some early classes on the Fairey Battle, all RCAF pilots (single engine guys) took their Service (advanced) Training on Harvards. Those on twins used Ansons and Cranes. One station I was on had some Yales (NA-64) with French instrumentation, to fly students before Harvards.

"The Harvard was easy to transition to if the primary training had been done in Tiger Moths or Fleets. Coming off the Cornells it could be difficult, as the Cornell was just too pleasant and easy to fly—not enough practice in keeping straight. The Mk. I Harvard was quite a different flying machine from the Mk. II. The Mk. I had a wing-dropping characteristic at the stall that forced one to treat it with respect. The RAF fixed theirs with slots with not much effect.

"During my later war years I was at CFS Trenton where the sole NA-44 was kept for VIP transport. It was similar in all respects to the Mk. I Harvard except for its 890 hp Cyclone and three-bladed prop, which made a most pleasant and musical sound to those on the ground. I enjoyed flying this sole example on trips.

"In my 2200 hours flying Mk. II Harvards I went all over the Prairies (at 40° below), up to Hudson's Bay and Eastern maritimes in squadron formations, in England and Scotland in some pretty grim weather, and in my Reserve days after the war, in conjunction with our Vampires.

"I also did a lot of low level aerobatics in the Harvard (and the Vamp), especially during airshows and county fairs, where the Canadian taxpayers could see their air force. Also did much three plane (leader) formation aerobatics while in the Reserve, with two other crazy guys in so close I was always afraid to look around, fear I would wiggle a little. In fact, during loops, I'd

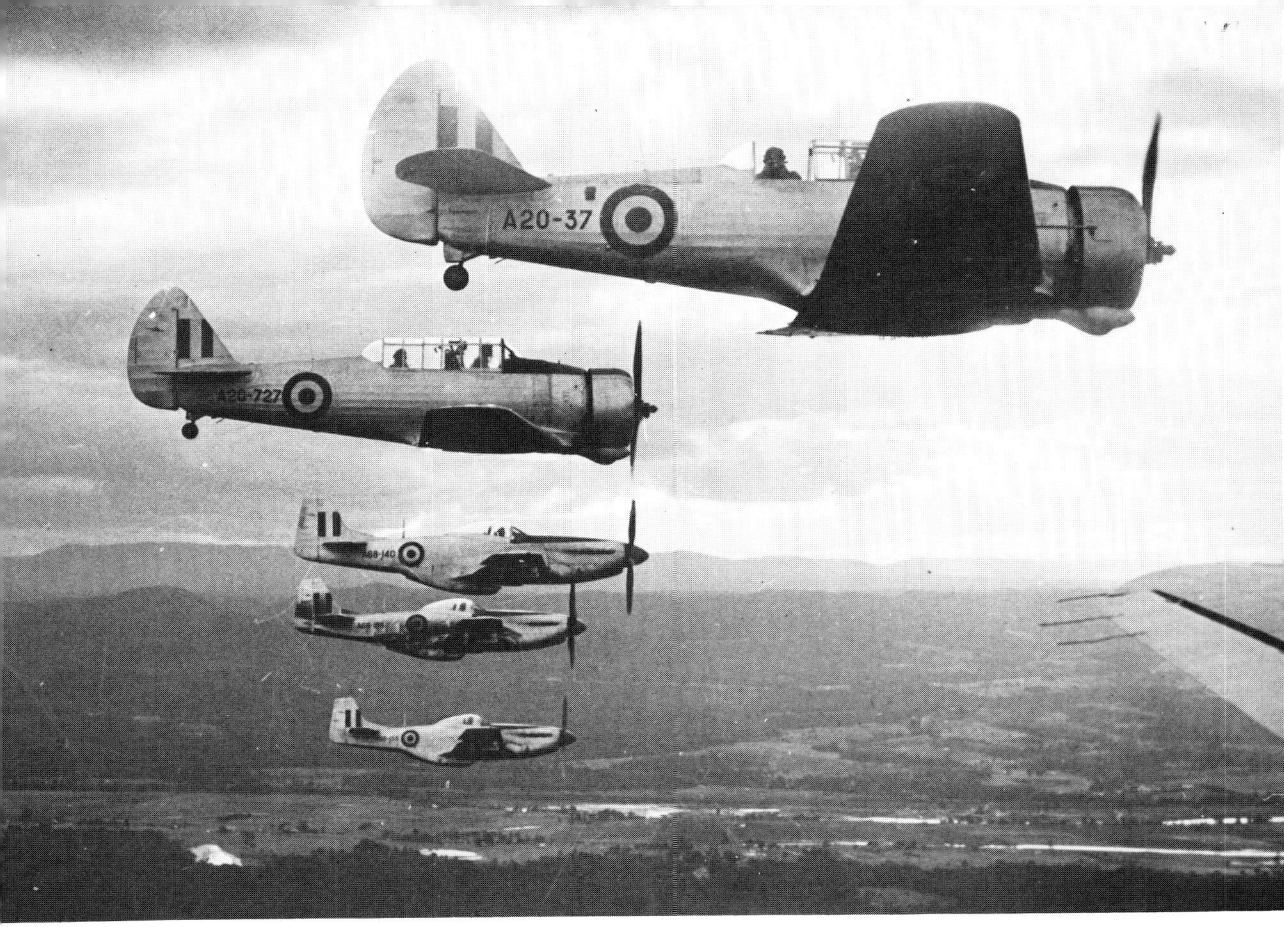

Top
Commonwealth Aircraft Corporation built not only the Wirraway under license but also the Mustang. Here Wirras lead a flight during a fly-past for the governor of New South Wales in 1952. The Mustangs are from No. 22 (City of Sydney) (Fighter) Squadron—the center Mustang with the oil streaks was flown by Milton Cottee, who got carried away doing an aerobatics sequence for the event. *(Dave Hudson)*

Bottom
An RAF Harvard IIB carrying practice bombs during postwar training. *(John Underwood)*

always prefer to start into the sun, so that over the top I could check station-keeping by the shadows on the ground, without turning my head.

"I feel I could have gone anywhere through most anything in the Harvard—snow, freezing rain, and that big heater was on six months of every year.

"I well recall, t'was back in 1943, my second tour at CFS Trenton. The C.O., Wing Commander J. G. Twist, A.F.C., was giving us the benefit of his experience at an instructor's meeting one day. He was harping on spinning, specifically the Mk. II Harvard, and warning us of dire consequences from waiting too long and too low before starting recovery. We had heard that the U.S. Air Corps did not spin the AT-6. Anyway, in the course of the diatribe, he slipped in the choice fact that at least the Mk. II would not spin inverted. (Some background here—about this time, a number of our Fleet trainers at the schools had been stalled inverted and spun in).

"You guessed it. Ten minutes after he said the Mk. II wouldn't spin inverted, 20 clowns were up there, making a monkey out of him. Comparing notes afterward (with the other clowns) it seems that inverted spin entries were indeed difficult—the aeroplane just didn't want to cooperate. It would appear initially as though it was falling out, and if pro-spin control was relaxed even a tiny bit, it would. This is why the boss probably said what he did.

"I have never found negative G to be anything but uncomfortable in any aircraft, and in the inverted Harvard it really was a case of grimly hanging on. Eventually it would spin inverted and go around quite smoothly, with everything falling up off the floor and the pee-tubes emptying all over you.

"Now I hasten to say that the Mk. II Harvard would only spin inverted to the pilot's right, or looking at it from another aeroplane or the ground, a left spin. If an inverted spin to the pilot's left was attempted, apparently the left offset fin would thwart all efforts, and being kindly, maybe this was why old Twist couldn't get the damn thing to go around."

The Harvard IIB assigned to Prince Philip, husband of Queen Elizabeth. Here the Prince flies over his home at Windsor Castle in 1953. *(John Underwood)*

A flight of Harvard MK-IIAs of 28 EFTS Mt. Hampton, Southern Rhodesia formate over the African countryside in 1944. *(Frank Smith)*

After World War II, as in the U.S., the Harvard was extensive use in most of the countries that had placed the aircraft in a key training role. In the RCAF the Harvard not only continued to come out of the factory as a new airframe, but it was considered essential to fighter transition training. Tom Patterson of 402 Squadron remembers that sequence flying in the aircraft was necessary before flying Vampires—much formation work, gunnery and aerobatics. "After flying Harvards we went on to conversion to the Vampires. We took the ground school conversion on 7-8 July 1949 and the ones who passed it, which was everybody, went to a Harvard with a regular force pilot which at that time was Flt Lt Wood.

"I was up with him in a Harvard and we would do a high speed landing . . . a very high speed landing; that's all there was. In the morning I signed my name to sign out a Vampire, walked up to the aircraft, climbed in and fired it up, and I was gone." Harvards were still a part of the squadron after Vamp conversion and on 17 September 1950 Tom took part in the Battle of Britain flight, with all-Harvard mass formation flying over Winnipeg. When 402 converted to Mustangs in 1951, the Harvard was again used for training and check rides.

As new Harvard IVs continued to be built in Canada in the early 1950s, pilots from many Commonwealth nations continued to get their flight training in the bird. Jeff Brown came to Canada as an RAF gunner who was accepted for flight training as an RAF officer . . . "The first two weeks were spent in ground school, everything being very 'Americanised,' lots of training films were used, many of them being genuine Walt Disney productions for the U.S. forces. The classrooms were equipped with steel framed chairs which had a wooden, overhanging desk top attached to the right hand side, just like the American high school classrooms which we had seen in films. I don't think anyone would have been surprised if Andy Hardy had walked in!

"To our surprise we found that unlike our colleagues who had remained in the U.K. to train, we were not due to do a preliminary training on a light aircraft but would do an all through course on the Harvard—the school was equipped with Mk. IIBs and some of the newer Mk. IVs. When seated in the cockpit for the first time the mass of instruments confronting you looked rather daunting and after the first bumbling attempts to run through the cockpit drills we began to wonder if we would ever master them properly.

"My group were greeted by a pleasant faced officer who with slightly greying hair looked somewhat middleaged; we later found out that he had been a Halifax 'driver' during the war, operating from a base in Yorkshire. . . . Our first trip was a one hour familiarisation flight to show us the district and to demonstrate the Harvard. . . . I had the hood open during the run up and the 600 horses of the Pratt & Whitney engine produced a head-splitting noise the like of which I had never experienced before. On one of my early attempts at doing a run up I became somewhat confused during the mag check and managed to get both magneto switches in the off position at the same time; quickly realising my mistake I slammed them both on together. During the short time that the engine had been 'freewheeling' the exhaust system had filled with unburnt mixture and the resultant explosion as the engine fired again must have been heard all over the field; this was immediately followed by

Top

During Israel's War of Independence in 1948, two AT-6s were bought in the U.S. and were adapted as attack fighters for dive bombing and ground support. They could carry up to eight bombs totaling 400 pounds or eight rockets or two .50 caliber machine guns mounted under the wings and one flexible .30 caliber operated by the "bombardier" in the rear seat. Numerous other T-6s and Harvards were bought for training and some were pressed into combat in 1956 but they were badly mauled by Egyptian antiaircraft. The trainers served until 1965. *(Israel Defense Forces)*

Center & bottom

A brand new AT-6A being readied at the factory for a delivery to China. *(NASM)*

A Royal Canadian Navy Harvard II serving the fleet in the early 1950s. *(Collect-Air Photos)*

Bombs Away! Six practice bombs fall from this RCAF Harvard II of the early '50s which also was equipped with rocket rails for air-to-ground weapons delivery training. *(NASM)*

a secondary explosion from the rear cockpit which was the instructor asking me what the hell I thought I was doing!

"We quickly found that taxying the Harvard was not as easy as it looked; the cowling of the bulky radial engine completely obscured any direct forward view and one had to taxi zig-zag fashion looking alternately to left and right of the nose. . . . The flying took place both at Claresholm and the relief field at Fort Macleaod some 10 miles to the south. Claresholm had twin parallel runways, one used for take offs and the other for landings in order to speed up the traffic flow—the whole place was like a giant bee hive with all yellow Harvards buzzing around all day and most nights."

Soon Brown was up for his first solo flight—"For some unknown reason I had taken off with the top open and was now hearing some unfamiliar propeller and engine noises; in addition to that it had started to rain and I found all this rather distracting so I decided to close the hood. I found that being tightly strapped in I was unable to twist round far enough to reach the release handle. I didn't want to undo the seat harness so I held the control column between my knees and made several unsuccessful grabs at it. All this time I was wallowing around the circuit and as it was now getting time to turn my attention to thoughts of landing I abandoned the idea and left the top open.

"My first approach was OK but I failed to get the aircraft into the correct 'three point' landing attitude and touched down on the main wheels only; this caused me to bounce so I applied full power and overshot. My instructor had always drummed into me the rule that if you were not sure of the landing and had sufficient gas, go around again—I was not taking any chances. My second attempt was similar to the first with not quite such a high bounce. I overshot again and yet again after the third attempt. The tower then called me up to ask if I required any assistance; politely refusing their offer I came in again and made quite a good landing. After taxying in I was met by the flight reception committee who grabbed me as I climbed out of the aircraft and with a large pair of scissors ceremonially cut off my tie at the knot—such was the custom on first solos at 3 F.T.S. The tie was chalked with name, date, position on course to go solo and then stapled to the wall of the crew room in line with the others.

"Some of the others were less fortunate—one unlucky lad had three attempts to go solo. Each time, as his reputation grew, he acquired a bigger and bigger audience of pupils and instructors who assembled to watch when the news went round that 'X' was going solo again. Three times he obligingly ground looped before the spectators, finally removing an undercarriage from the aircraft. . . . He was then 'washed out.'

"The training progressed from general handling to aerobatics, instrument and formation flying and navigation exercises. The Harvard with its 2½ tons gross weight and 600 hp engine, could be quite a handful for the would-be throttle jockey and with its strong tendency to swing on take off and landing, ground looping was a daily occurrence."

As more new Mk. IVs came out of the Canadian Car & Foundry factory in the early 1950s, the market for the aircraft did not seem to suffer. West Germany received new Harvard Mk-4s from the Canadian Car and Foundry Company in 1956, then used them in training school at Furstenfeldbrück until 1966. Charlie Hubbs "picked up about 1300 hours in T-6/Harvards, mostly Harvards, from 1954 to 1957 when the German Air Force was just starting up again. As their American flight instructors, the 7330th Flying Training Wing was set up at Furstenfeldbrück near Munich.

Opposite page top two photos
SK-16s of the Swedish Air Force in the early 1950's. *(Lars Olausson)*

SK-16A. 16706 of the Swedish Air Force, 1953. *(Lars Olausson)*

Below
The second T-6J built by the Canadian Car & Foundry company from the Harvard IV line. Six of these aircraft went to the USAF to replace six T-6Ds lost while on loan to the RCAF. *(John Underwood)*

One of the Harvard IVs built as a T-6J under U.S. contract for delivery to West Germany as a part of the Military Assistance Program. Upon this aircraft was built the beginnings the new Luftwaffe in the 1950s. *(Georg Fischbach via Pete Bowers)*

A busy 1953 flight line scene of SK-16s of the Swedish Air Force, Primary Training School F5 Ljungbyhed. Sweden was one of the major users of this type after World War II. *(Lara Olavsson)*

A Swedish Air Force SK-16A on display at Uppsala Sweden, June 1968. *(Jim Sullivan)*

"We picked up brand new Harvards (1-1½ hours on them) off ships at Belfast, Ireland. We ferried them to Germany and had, I believe, 120 planes for only 28 instructors. When the program slipped a little we just had to fly hell out of those nice new planes—all over Europe. Of course since the Harvard could land anywhere, it was routine to go to Nice, Corsica, Monaco, Majorca—really tough.

"I put one in a football field once in a rain storm and I really thought I could do it. It was an emergency run and they had taken the goal posts down so I could get a priest into a no landing strip site. The Harvard was going faster off the far end than what I touched down at. On another emergency run to get a doc to a hurt guy on the gunnery range; I got the bird in, but we had to use the fireman's axes to cut down enough trees so I could get out.

"A lieutenant friend of mine, practicing forced landings, hit the only tree for 20 miles (student never said a word about the tree—IP couldn't see it from the backseat). They knocked the right wing off and did some fast rolls for a quarter mile or so. Finally crashed with worst injury a chipped tooth."

Altogether some 50 countries around the world would use the plane in their training plans both during World War II and long after. The aircraft's versatility and adaptability became readily apparent to most of the major air forces of the world, making the design the most widely used training aircraft ever.

During the war years, in addition to the tremendous training programs being carried on in the U.S. and Canada, a large training unit was established in Rhodesia using basically 700 Harvard IIA aircraft. These aircraft served throughout the war and well into the 1960s.

Sweden expanded its use of the series after the war and in addition to the SK-16s already in strength, they acquired 257 more aircraft including SNJ-2s, AI-6As, BC-1As, SNJ-3s and a considerable number of SNJ-4s from U.S. surplus stocks.

With the formation of NATO, initial batches of Royal Navy and RAF Harvards were used in the restructuring of NATO air arms including Norwegian, Danish, Belgian and Dutch forces. Considerable numbers of AT-6s and SNJs from U.S. stocks also went to Portugal, Spain, Italy, Greece, France, Turkey and Germany. As part of an effort to beef-up their air forces, SNJs were supplied to Japan, Taiwan and the Philippines.

Holland, which was one of the major users of the T-6/Harvard series after WWII, had strength of 240 of the aircraft with 40 sent to the Netherlands East Indies Air Force. These planes were later transferred to Indonesia and finally withdrawn in 1966.

Below
A T-6G of the Philippine Air Force reposes on the line at Clark Field, P.I. *(Dave Menard)*

Opposite page top to bottom
A lineup of Mexican Air Force AT-6Ds at the Military Aviation School, Zapapan, Jalisco near Guadalajara. (Mexican Air Force Base #5) Mexico has been the most consistent user of the type having had them on strength since the early 1940s. *(Santiago Flores Ruiz)*

One of the first 27 T-6s delivered to Chile from surplus stocks in the U.S. *(USAF)*

Well maintained Venezuelan AT-6s on the line in 1950. Notice the hard rubber tailwheels. *(Harry Gann)*

777
751

EA
239

Opposite page top to bottom
A Royal New Zealand Air Force AT-6D makes a low pass over Wigram Air Field during the aerobatic display to commemorate 36 years of RNZAF Harvard service. Piloting the plane is Wing CDR. Don McAllister, MBE. *(RNZAF)*

A Harvard in the Indian Air Force of the 1950s. *(USAF)*

Royal Thai Air Force T-6s at Korat Air Base, Thailand, on January 22, 1969. The Thais had three groups of T-6s in service until the '70s. *(USAF)*

Another Thai T-6D carrying colorful markings on a silver painted airframe.

AT-6s of the Royal New Zealand Air Force performing as an aerobatic team, complete with smoke. *(John Underwood)*

On 24 June 1977, the RNZAF retired their remaining AT-6s and Harvards after 36 years of faithful service. Here on the flight line at RNZAF Base Wigram, 18 planes of the Flying Training Wing prepare to taxi out for their final flight. A number of these planes were from the original batch of lend-lease AT-6Ds received in World War II. *(RNZAF)*

15

HT275
8

4302

As surplus AT-6s, SNJs and Harvards continued to fly in overseas air forces, they were pressed into light attack roles with bomb racks and forward firing guns. The Spanish Air Force used several squadrons of T-6s as C6s with two 7.7 mm Breda machine guns and 12 Oerlikon air-to-ground underwing rockets or 10 221 pound bombs. At the beginning of World War II the Mexican Air Force caught a German submarine on the surface—an AT-6 is reported to have divebombed and sunk it. The Brazilian Air Force operated several T-6s in the attack role into the early 1970s and their Texan aerial demonstration team was popular all over South America.

In the era immediately following World War II, the French established flying schools in Morocco where large numbers of Harvards and T-6s were used. The Algerian uprising of 1954 sparked the largest use of that type of aircraft in a combat environment. Although armed T-6s have been used in various small conflicts, it was in the mid-50s French Colonial War in North Africa that T-6s were used in the greatest numbers during the armed counter insurgency role. The French Air Force received an additional 150 T-6Gs for this purpose early in 1956 with an additional 150 later during the same year, and was operating about 600 of all types by 1958. Among these were a considerable number of SNJs acquired from USN stocks.

Spanish Air Force C.6 Attack aircraft performing as a military aerobatic team. These MAP-supplied T-6Gs has provisions for two 7.7 mm wing guns and ten 10 kg bombs or 12 rockets. French and Portugese T-6Gs had bomb racks and mountings for external gun pods. *(John Underwood)*

Brazil's Esquadrilla da Fumaca (Squadron of Smoke), one of the more popular aerobatic teams in South America at the time. The letters F.A.B. were the initials of the Brazilian Air Force in Portugese. *(Juan Arraez Cerda via John Underwood)*

Japanese SNJ-6s which were supplied to the JNASDF by the U.S. Navy to get Japan back in the air after World War II. *(Hideya Ando via Pete Bowers)*

A T-6F of the Japanese Air Self-Defense Force on September 29, 1962, at Misawa Air Base. T-6s and SNJs proved invaluable to Japan in getting former pilots requalified and new pilots trained for its growing air forces in the 1950s and '60s. *(Dave Menard)*

In the late 1950s, it was the T-6 series which bore the brunt of combat operations during the Algerian campaign. Armament usually included internal wing guns, two 7.5mm gun pads under the wings with 300 rounds per gun, napalm tanks, 50 pound bombs, four small bombs under each wing or two packs of seven 68mm rockets. The T-28 gradually replaced the T-6 operationally, but some remained until 1962 when the war ended. The remaining T-6/Harvard types were used as training aircraft until withdrawn in 1966.

Africa was a continual source of combat for the aircraft as countries struggled in one war after the other through the 1960s and 1970s.

Many of the Belgian T-6s and Harvards were sent to Belgian Congo for use at Kamina training school. In July of 1960 they were hastily armed and used to put down the newly independent Congolese Republic rebellion.

Portugal operated a considerable number of Harvards and AT-6s until recently. Some of the Portuguese Harvards, which were received from the SAAF for use in Africa, armed with bombs and machine guns, were used in anti-guerilla operations over Angola in 1961. Similar operations occurred in Portuguese Guinea.

When the eastern region of Nigeria ceded under the name of The Republic of Biafra, T-6s were once again involved in a shooting war. Only about 12 T-6s were known to be involved, but the venerable warrior proved once again that it was capable of the task. Attack versions of the aircraft were spotted in these areas as late as 1980.

The 50th anniversary of the NA-16 design will be in 1985. At least 14 countries will still be flying this type of aircraft for various duties. South Africa is the largest user with 50 planes on hand. In Latin America, the T-6 variants not only serve as trainers but as armed reconnaissance aircraft as well. It appears this great aircraft will be serving faithfully well past its 50th anniversary.

As the Vietnam war heated up in the early 1960s, Laos made heavy use of armed T-6s, using rockets and guns to fly combat.

The last attempt by North American to sell the Texan to the U.S. took the form of this FT-6G counterinsurgency (COIN) version which was tested at Edwards AFB, California, in the late 1950s. With bombs, gun pods and external fuel or napalm, it was quite a formidable machine for a T-6 but the day of the Texan had already passed. *(Harry Gann)*

The end of the line—one of the last T-6Gs at Davis-Monthan AFB. Arizona, in June 1972, still in storage. *(Roy Lock/Bruce Orriss via AAHS)*

Chapter Five

The Texan Flies On

Today North American's famous trainer is being restored in ever increasing numbers by devoted enthusiasts and the great formations of the past are once again taking shape for airshow crowds. Here (from bottom to top) Fred Webster in a Harvard IV, Pete Vandersluis in a T-6G, Dan Dameo in a T-6D and Jerry Walbrun in an SNJ-5 fly as members of Warbirds of America. *(Jeff Ethell)*

As the 1980s stretch into history, the popularity of the AT-6 has, if anything, increased, only this time with civilian owners. Not only have the aircraft been raced, stripped of all nonessential weight, but they have been restored back to pristine condition by loving enthusiasts in such organizations as Warbirds of America, the T-6 Owners Association and many others. The long vanished parade reviews at Randolph Pensacola and numerous other military training fields have returned as pilots fly together in tight 20 plus formations for the benefit of those who never saw such sights.

A trip to the Warbirds of America flight line at the Annual EAA Fly In at Oshkosh, Wisconsin, will reward the T-6/Harvard enthusiast with the sight of at least 50 of these planes all neatly lined up in one place. The restoration encompasses every series of AT-6, SNJ or Harvard and owners spend considerable time and much money to be certain the planes are cared for. An organization known as the T-6 Owners Association has blossomed into being during the past few years and has helped spark continued interest in the T-6 as a Pacing Class of airplanes at the National Air Races, Reno, Nevada, and as a bonafide antique airplane in the Warbird category.

The Warbirds of America, with assistance from the T-6 Owners Association, has conducted safety seminars in the maintenance and operation of the Texan series for the past five years, thereby passing an awareness to the owners that helps to insure longevity of the airplanes. A static airplane in a museum is one thing—one this old that still flies regularly is something else.

A surprising number are currently active in the U.S. The breakdown of planes still on the U.S. civil register include 12 rather rare SNJ-2s, the bulk of which are currently earning their keep in the skywriting business. There are also 22 AT-6A-SNJ-3 series, 3 AT-6Bs, 73 AT-6C-SNJ-4s, 82 AT-6Ds-SNJ-5s, 68 AT-6Fs-SNJ-6s, 3 SNJ-7s, 6 Harvard Mk-IIs, 10 Harvard Mk-IVs and 105 T-6Gs. At this writing, the total varies between 385–400 currently active at any one time. Not included in this total are the non-flying museum aircraft, the planes licensed in Canada, and an estimated 50 more throughout the U.S. and Canada that exist in derelict condition.

An increasing number of Harvards have appeared on the civil register in Europe. Almost every yearly aerial display in the U.K. produces a variety of Harvards in various color schemes. Recently, the air forces of Italy, Spain, Sweden and Portugal have declared the last of their Harvards surplus and many of these machines have found their way to proud owners in Norway, Sweden, Switzerland, and UK, Holland and France.

It appears that North America's incredible trainer, the greatest of all global pilot makers, will be around for some time to come. The familiar drone of its engine has not yet disappeared from the skies—this historic warbird will be around as long as there is fuel to power it.

N66J

Opposite page top to center

The Bacon Super T-6S was the last major modification undertaken on the T-6, done by Gordon Israel in 1957. Major efforts were taken to clean the airframe up and reduce frontal area, resulting in a cruise of 216 mph at 10,000 feet with 64% power—the stock T-6 normally cruised at 170 mph. *(Pete Bowers)*

What is bound to be the only T-6 biplane ever flown was built by Bob Stroop from two SNJ-5s for crop dusting. Upper wings were bolted together outer wing panels and all four ailerons worked, while the chemical tank was an old belly tank stuffed into the rear cockpit. No canopy, of course, Duster J. F. Carter of Monroeville, Alabama, bought it and will never forget flying it—"anything below 23" and 1800 rpm and she would start settling. Was terribly slow, gear was kept down, best I remember never indicated over 90 kts full bore. I'm no engineer, but it had too, way too much lifting area. As soon as the tail would come up it would fly . . . maybe 200 feet if you held it down. It would descend like a helicopter and the engine would check descent but Lord help you if that engine ever sputtered." *(J. F. Carter)*

Opposite page bottom

This "Thunderbolt" is typical of the many modifications made to the basic T-6 airplane to make the machine resemble something else. Apparently, the T-6/Harvard series typifies all the round engined aircraft of World War II. Here, a Harvard sits patiently awaiting its cue to play a P-47 or "something" in the movie "A Bridge Too Far." *(R. Bonser)*

Below

Interest in the type has increased in England in recent years. This gathering of Harvards occurred at Bassingbourn in May 1978. *(R. Bonser)*

A number of ex-Portuguese Harvards have found their way to new owners in the U.K. This Harvard was at Bassingbourn. *(R. Bonser)*

Top

Considered to be one of the finest AT-6 restorations in the U.S. is Warbirds of America Director John Harrison's AT-6A-NA (the fifth AT-6A built) based in the Sacramento, California area. The plane is finished in the markings of the 94th Pursuit Squadron, a fitting tribute to the most significant training aircraft ever built. *(Bill Larkins)*

Bottom

One of the finest and most authentic restorations of an ex-Navy SNJ. This SNJ-5 Ex BuNo. 43817 is owned by Warbirds of America and Experimental Aircraft Association Director Jerry Walbrun. Like John Harrison's AT-6, the plane has been restored to pristine condition and is so maintained. In addition to its regular appearance at shows, this ship has been the lead plane in the mass formation fly-bys at Oshkosh each year. *(Jim Sullivan)*

Top
These SNJ-2s are still earning their keep by skytyping. Sponsored by the Miller Brewing Co. and known as the Miller Squadron, 6 SNJ-2s operated by Skytypers East, Flushing, N.Y., type messages in the sky 1,000 ft. high and 4 to 6 miles long advertising the Miller Product. The planes fly line abreast, the smoke in each plane being triggered by a computer in the lead ship. Each plane in turn emits a series of smoke puffs which appear as letters when viewed from the ground.

Bottom
Jerry Walbrun leads this flight of beautifully restored trainers over Oshkosh. Following the SNJ-5 are Dan Dameo in his AT-6D, Pete Vandersluis in the T-6G and Fred Webster in a Harvard MK IV. *(Photo by Jeff Ethell)*

VERSION TABLE

Type	Engine	Elect Syst.	Armament: Guns	Armament: Bombs	Camera Prov.	Tailwheel	Tail Hook	Aove Rear Hood	Rudder	Wing Tips	Wing Span
BC-1	R-1340-47	12V				steerable		no	round	round	42′7″
BC-1A	R-1340-47	12V				steerable		yes	triang	square	42′¼″
AT-6	R-1340-47	12V				steerable		yes	triang	square	42′¼″
AT-6A	R-1340-49	12V	cowl, rear		gun	steerable		yes	triang	square	42′¼″
AT-6B	R-1340-49	12V	cowl, rear		gun	steerable		yes	triang	square	42′¼″
AT-6C	R-1340-AN-1	12V	cowl, rear, wing	yes	gun, vert	steerable		yes	triang	square	42′¼″
AT-6D	R-1340-AN-1	24V	cowl, rear, wing	yes	gun, vert	steerable		yes	triang	square	42″¼″
AT-6F*	R-1340-AN-1	24V	cowl, wing		gun	steerable		no	triang	square	42′¼″
T-6G	R-1340-AN-1	24V	(only LT-6G)**			steering/locking		no	triang	square	42′¼″
T-6H	R-1340-CRMA	24V				steering/locking		no	triang	square	42′¼″
T-6J	R-1340-CRMA	24V				steering/locking		no	triang	square	42′¼″
A-27	R-1820-75	24V	cowl, rear, wing	yes		steerable		yes	triang	square	42′¼″
AT-16	R-1340-49	24V	cowl			steerable		yes	triang	square	42′¼″
P-64	R-1820-77	24V	nose, wing	yes		steerable		no	triang	square	37′3″
SNJ-1	R-1340-6	12V				lockable		no	round	round	42′7″
SNJ-2	R-1340-36	12V				lockable		no	round	square	42″7″
SNJ-3	R-1340-AN-1	12V	cowl, rear		vert	steerable (C-lock)	C only	yes	triang	square	42′¼″
SNJ-4	R-1340-AN-1	12V	cowl, rear, wing	yes	gun, vert	steerable*** (C-lock)	C only	yes	triang	square	42′¼″
SNJ-5	R-1340-AN-1	24V	cowl, rear, wing	yes	gun, vert	steerable*** (C-lock)	C only	yes	triang	square	42′¼″
SNJ-6*	R-1340-AN-1	24V	cowl		gun	Steerable*** (C-lock)	C only	no	triang	square	42′¼″
SNJ-7	R-1340-AN-1	24V	wing (B only)		gun	lockable	C only	no	triang	square	42′¼″
Harvard I	R-1340-S3H1	12V				steerable		no	round	round	42′7″
Harvard II	R-1340-49****	12V	rockets	yes		steerable		no	triang	square	42′¼″
Harvard III	R-1340-AN-1	12V	rockets	yes		steerable		no	triang	square	42′¼″
Harvard IV	R-1340-AN-1	24V				steering/locking		no	triang	square	42′¼″
Wirraway	R-1340-S1H1	12V	cowl, rear	yes		steerable			round	round	42′7″

*Only models with belly bank provisions

**LT-6G built for Korea with rocket racks; COIN versions later modified with minigun pods and bomb racks.

***Later modified to lockable.

****IIA was lend-lease model of AT-6A; IIB was license-built in Canada with USAAF designation AT-16 by Noorduyn. IV built in early 1950s by Canadian Car & Foundry. Wirraway license-built in Australia by Commonwealth Aircraft Company.

GLOSSARY

AAB	U.S.N. Aircraft Armament Bulletin
ASC	U.S.N. Aircraft Service Change
ATD	Aviation Training Detachment
ATU, BTU	Post War Naval designation for training squadrons, i.e. Advance Training Unit, Basic Training Unit
CQTU	Carrier Qualification Training Unit
Fox-Corpen	Carriers compass heading for the launching and recovery of aircraft
VA	Fleet designation for a U.S.N. Attack Squadron
VB or VSB	Fleet designation for a U.S.N. Bombing Squadron or Scout/Bombing Squadron
VC or VU	Fleet designation for a Composite or Utility squadron
VF	Fleet designation for a U.S.N. Fighter Squadron
VN Detachment	Fleet Night Fighter detachment. Usually a small group specializing in Night Tactics—attached to an Air Group
VN3D8	Naval designation for a typical Navy training squadron, i.e. Training Squadron 3
VS	Fleet designation for a U.S.N. Scouting Squadron
VT	Fleet designation for a U.S.N. Torpedo Squadron
V-5/V-12	WWII and post war U.S.N. college training programs which would eventually result in flight training and designation as a Naval Aviator

BIBLIOGRAPHY

Andrade, John M. US MILITARY AIRCRAFT DESIGNATIONS AND SERIALS SINCE 1909. Midland Counties Publications. Leicester: 1979.

Bell, Dana. AIR FORCE COLORS, Vols. 1 & 2. Squadron/Signal Publications. Carrollton: 1979, 1980.

Cline, Maj. Tim, USAF. "The Airborne FAC in the Korean War." AAHS JOURNAL, Vol. 21, No. 4 (Winter 1976), pp. 257-262.

deVries, Col. John A., USAF (Ret). "North American AT-6/SNJ 'Texan.' " HISTORICAL AVIATION ALBUM, Vol. XVI, 1980, pp. 35-55.

Doll, Thomas E. US NAVY MARKINGS, WWII PACIFIC THEATER. John W. Caler Corp. Sun Valley: 1967.

Kohn, Leo. THE STORY OF THE TEXAN. Aviation Publications. Milwaukee: 1975.

Krauskopf, Robert. "National Guard Aviation—1940-41." AAHS JOURNAL, Vol. 5, No. 1 (Spring 1960), pp. 14-19.

Morgan, Len. THE AT-6 HARVARD. Arco Publishing Co. New York: 1965.

Risedorph, Gene. "Mosquito." AAHS JOURNAL, Vol. 24, No. 1 (Spring 1979), pp. 45-51.

Swanborough, Gordon. NORTH AMERICAN: AN AIRCRAFT ALBUM. Arco Publishing Co. New York: 1973.

Wolf, William, DDS. "USAF Pilot Training in World War II." HISTORICAL AVIATION ALBUM, Vol. XVI, 1980, pp. 56-62.